KEN WARREN TEACHES

TEXAS HOLD'EM

2

ABOUT THE AUTHOR

Ken Warren has supported himself playing professional poker since he left the Air Force in 1987, and has parlayed that success into a career as one of the best-selling poker authors of all time. He has written five other books on poker, including *Winner's Guide to Texas Hold'em Poker* and *The Big Book of Poker*. Warren is the best of the new breed of riverboat poker players, and has the unique distinction of playing in and winning the very first legal poker hand in Mississippi in the 20th century. That landmark hand was kings full of sevens in the big blind position.

KEN WARREN TEACHES

TEXAS HOLD'EM 2

KEN WARREN

CARDOZA PUBLISHING

See Free Book Offer On Page 304

Cardoza Publishing is the foremost gaming and gambling publisher in the world with a library of over 200 up-to-date and easy-to-read books and strategies. These authoritative works are written by the top experts in their fields and with more than 10 million books in print, represent the best-selling and most popular gaming books anywhere.

Library of Congress Catalog No: 2008938505
ISBN 10: 1-58042-254-3
ISBN 13: 978-1-58042-254-3

Visit our new web site (www.cardozabooks.com) or write us for a full list of books, advanced and computer strategies.

CARDOZA PUBLISHING
P.O. Box 98115, Las Vegas, NV 89193
Toll Free Phone (800) 577-WINS
email: cardozabooks@aol.com
www.cardozabooks.com

CONTENTS

I dedicate this book to my mother,
Dolores Shirley Rich Warren

BOOKS BY KEN WARREN

Winner's Guide to Texas Hold'em Poker

Ken Warren Teaches Texas Hold'em (Volume I)

Ken Warren Teaches Texas Hold'em (Volume II)

Ken Warren Teaches 7-Card Stud

Winners Guide to Omaha Poker

The Big Book of Poker

1.
INTRODUCTION

I didn't see you make the final table in the World Series of Poker (WSOP) last year. And you know what? You didn't see me there, either. That's because you and I both are not rich, superstar poker players who make appearances on television year in and year out and play in the big games where hundreds of thousands of dollars change hands daily.

And that's why the concepts and strategies I talk about here can help you. This book is intended to be of help to the average limit hold'em player who plays in $2/$4 games up to $10/$20. I will give you a fresh perspective on the game to take you from loser to winner. But first, let me ask you a few questions:

Are you...
- Tired of being busted out of the game after just an hour or two, or even after a bunch of hours?

- Tired of not going home with extra money in your pocket and a smile on your face?

- Tired of not getting the cards you need to win?

- Tired of having your blinds stolen from you?

- Tired of watching all that action going on around you and being the only player at your table to not win a hand?

- Tired of not being able to build your stack like the best player at the table?

If this describes your typical hold'em experience, it's because you're making too many simple, basic mistakes that can easily be corrected. Get ready to leave all that tiredness in the past, because Ken Warren has taken aim at your hold'em game and the winner is going to be you! You can make money at hold'em — but to join the winner's circle, you need to learn a few things. I'm here to help you do that.

My Approach

This book begins with the assumption that you already know how to play poker and you are interested in learning how to play Texas hold'em. Perhaps you already know a little about hold'em and you're looking to increase both your skill and your profit at the game.

There are two prevalent methods of teaching students new material. One way is called the lecture method, wherein the teacher talks, the students listen and take notes, and there is nothing else to be said or done by either party. You could say that reading a book is the same as attending a written lecture. The second method of teaching students new material is called the discussion method. This is where the teacher introduces a subject to be taught, the student thinks about it and tries to learn the material, and then asks for clarification, further explanation, examples, or a restatement of the concept in different words. It is a back-and-forth discussion that follows the subject matter that is being taught. It is a question and answer session that allows the student to ask all of the questions he needs to in order to be able to fully grasp and understand the material being taught.

This book is borne out of recognition of the fact that sometimes a simple lecture is not enough, especially for a complicated subject like Texas hold'em. Perhaps you're old enough to recall the book, *Everything You Always Wanted to Know About Sex* (*But Were Afraid to Ask)*, by Dr. David Reuben, published back in the 1960s. It's probably the greatest discussion-method book ever written.

I first saw the book when I was a twelve-year-old riding the cheesewagon (yellow school bus) to school. It didn't have anyone who claimed ownership; it was the bus copy. All the kids would take turns reading it and passing it around during the ride to and from school, and then hiding it somewhere in the bus so we could pick up where we left off on the next bus ride. It was a great book and it had a positive influence on my life; however, I never would have thought it would influence me to write a book using the same method.

Thanks, Dr. Reuben, for more than one thing.

2.
BASIC STUFF

WHAT IS TEXAS HOLD'EM?

Texas hold'em is a poker game where the players are dealt two personal, face-down cards and five other cards are dealt face up in the middle of the table. You then use your best combination of all seven cards to make your final poker hand. The highest hand wins.

Is it easy to play?

Since you have only two cards in your hand, it's easy to make decisions and you'll usually be ready to act when it's your turn.

What else?

Since each player is dealt two cards face down and there are no other upcards at this point, that means that you don't have to remember or memorize the other player's upcards and the order in which they received them as you would in stud games. This saves a lot of time and allows you to expend your mental energy on other things.

Your betting position stays the same throughout the entire game. If you are first to act at the beginning of the hand, you will be first to act on every betting round during that hand. Likewise, if you are last to act, then you will be last for all four betting rounds.

What's an advantage of hold'em over 7-card stud?

The pots are usually bigger in hold'em than they are in stud when the players have the same strength hands. That's because a hold'em game is typically played nine- or ten-handed while stud games are played five- or six-handed. There are more players in the game to put more money in the pots because the hands are more competitive.

What do you mean by "more competitive"?

The final strength of all the remaining players' hands will be closer together in value than they would be in a stud game. That's because six different stud players can each hold seven different cards to make poker hands that could be wildly different from each other. Hands could range anywhere from no pair to a royal flush. One player could have a club flush while another player could have a heart flush. This doesn't happen in hold'em.

Why not?

Because even though each player has his own two private cards that belong to his poker hand only, there are going to be five more cards face up on the board that will belong to all of the players in the game. So, at the end of the hand, five-sevenths of your possible poker hand will also be five-sevenths of everyone else's hand. Since it's really only the difference between everyone's private cards that you're betting on, you can see that every players' final poker hand will be close in strength to the other players' hands.

So this makes the pots bigger?

Yes. When ten players begin a hand with two cards and then they get to share three more cards immediately, it makes for a game where there's a real contest for the money, there's a lot of betting, and the hands are close. This makes for bigger pots because more players are in the running from the beginning of the hand. It's not like stud, where every player sometimes gets a hand he should fold and one player wins the small ante.

How am I going to know when to play the hand or not?

As you will see in the "Hand Selection" chapter, certain hands (two-card combinations that you are going to be dealt) are already known to be winners in the long run and other certain hands are positively known to be losers. And, of course, there are a large number of hands in between where the answer to the question, "Should I play these hands?" is, "It depends."

How is this an advantage over other poker games?

The good thing about hold'em is that in the beginning of the game, the number of card combinations is relatively small. There are 1,326 different ways to combine any two cards from a deck of 52 cards but, if you discount similar hands (K♦ 6♠ is the same as K♣ 6♥), then there are only 169 possible two-card hands. A beginning player can easily be taught to play only certain hands while in certain positions at the beginning of the game.

Are there any more advantages to hold'em?
Absolutely. The community card nature of the game allows you to get a better feeling for the value of your hand versus that of your opponent and lets you know if it's okay to fold at each stage of the betting rounds if you think it's the right thing to do.

Is there one last, best reason that hold'em might be a better game than stud?
Yes. I'm glad you asked. And that is, in hold'em you *always* get to see your opponent's seventh and final card. It's called the *river card*. You'll always know if he could have made that flush or straight he was drawing for. This is not true in stud, because your opponent's final card is always face down.

HOW TO PLAY TEXAS HOLD'EM
There are some basic questions about the rules of the game and how the game is going to be conducted before you can deal the first hand.

How much money can I bet, and how do I do it?
Hold'em can be played for any limit you like, but all of the betting in a limit game follows one strict guideline: There are four betting rounds and the limit for the first two betting rounds is one unit and the limit for the third and fourth betting round is two units. This is called a 1 to 2 ratio.

Why is this so?

As the pot gets bigger, it is a necessary strategy to be able to bet more to protect your hands, to make it incorrect for other players to play against you, and to help emphasize the skill factor in poker.

How exactly does this 1 to 2 betting ratio thing work?

Assume you want to play with a highest bet limit of $4. The limit for the first two bets would be $2, and the limit for the last two bets would be $4. Hence, the 1 to 2 ratio. You must bet and raise exactly the predetermined amount for the appropriate betting round. This is the same formula for any amount. For example, there are also $5/$10, $10/$20, $15/$30, $1/$2 and many other limits.

Is the betting always like this?

No. Apparently, rules are made to be broken. Sometimes a hold'em game will be played with what's called *spread-limit*. That means you can bet any amount you like up to the maximum allowed for that betting round. The most popular spread-limit amount offered in public poker rooms is $1-$4-$8-$8. That means you can bet from $1 to $4 on the first two betting rounds and from $1 to $8 on the last two betting rounds. If you're first to bet, you always have the option of betting nothing, but that will be covered later.

What's this betting of all of your chips that I see on television?

That's called no-limit. That means you can bet any and all of your chips at any time and at any stage of any betting round during the game. No-limit truly means that there is no limit. Actually, that's not really true — you can only bet as many chips or as much money as you have in front of you at the beginning of the hand.

How do I play hold'em?

I will describe how hold'em is dealt in a casino poker room, since that's where most of you will play and that's what you see on television.

Because each player gets only two cards, hold'em can be played with as many as twenty-two players at the table! Or it can be played with only two players. This is not a solitary game. The most common number players to have in the game is nine or ten.

How do you start?

Everyone takes a seat and then the house dealer deals everyone one card face up to determine who has the dealer position for the first game. Highest card is it. That player is awarded a plastic button with the word "Dealer" on each side to indicate that he is in the dealer position for that hand. Every player at the table gets his turn in the rotation at the dealer's position — which is called the *button* — it's just that someone else will actually deal the cards for you.

What happens now?

The first player to the left of the button (the dealer's position) has to post what's called a *small blind*. The next player to his left has to post what's called a *big blind*. In a $2/$4 game, the small and big blinds would be $1 and $2, respectively.

The blinds are only the blinds for this hand. After the hand is over, the dealer button moves one player to the left and the blinds are posted by two different players. Since the deal rotates with every hand, every player will be in the blinds his fair share of the time and it averages out.

When does a player ante to get cards?

There is no ante in hold'em cash games. The blinds take the place of the antes and it's probably a good thing because it speeds up the game. There's no bickering over trying to figure out who the one player is who didn't ante, as in a stud game. In a way, the first two players ante for everybody.

How does play begin?

The first player to the immediate left of the big blind must act first. He can either fold, call, or raise the big blind. The next player, and each player after him in turn, must act based on the action required when it is his turn to act. If it is the small blind's turn to act and no one has raised, then he can either fold and forfeit the one-half bet he posted, call the other half of the bet to match the big blind's bet, or he can raise.

He can raise himself? I thought you couldn't do that in poker?

Ordinarily, you'd be right, but there's an exception in hold'em and other flop games. The players in the blinds only can raise themselves before the flop. This is to compensate them for the fact that they had to bet in the dark before they got their cards and to allow them the same right to raise as all the other players in the game. After the flop, the usual rule of not raising yourself applies.

What happens next?

After all of the players have acted on their two private cards, the dealer then *burns* one card (removes it from play) and then turns three cards face up on the board all at once. These cards belong to all of the players still in the hand. Those three cards are called the *flop*. The top card, or the burn card, is removed from play as a procedural caution against the possibility that it might have an identifying mark on it and therefore might be known to one of the players in the game. It's an old custom.

In the old days before plastic cards and scrupulously honest dealers, the value of a card might be known by any number of ways. It might have a mark on it as a result of normal use and wear. Or it might have been deliberately marked. It doesn't matter. The top card never comes into play on any round of hold'em. This prevents a player from playing his hand with the knowledge that the next card off the top of the deck to hit the board is going to be the 9♥ or any other card.

And then?

After the three flop cards hit the board, there is another round of betting, beginning with the first active player to the dealer's left. Every active player must act on his hand, even if it's to do nothing. A player who says "check" is actually saying, "I bet nothing." If there's a bet, all you have to do is think about that saying from the old West: "Your cards or your money." If you're facing a bet, you have to either put the money in the pot or surrender your cards.

So now each player has five cards. What's next?

The dealer then burns a card and turns only one card face up. This is called the *turn card*. There is another round of betting. The dealer then burns a final card and turns one last card face up on the board. This is called the *river card*. After all the action is finished after the fifth upcard, the hand is over. Anyone who wants to claim the pot has to turn his cards face up for all to see. The dealer has a duty to make a bona-fide good faith effort to read all face-up hands and award the pot to the winner.

Anything else I need to know to finish up a hand?

Yes. You always need to show both of your cards to win the pot, even if you're using only one of them to make your poker hand. Also, don't surrender your cards to the dealer until the dealer pushes you the pot. And don't forget to tip your dealer if you determine a tip is appropriate. More about tipping later.

I know how to play poker, but reading hands with community cards is new to me. Can you give me some examples?

Sure. You have two cards in your hand and five on the board, for a total of seven cards. You use the best combination of those seven cards to make your final five-card hand. The key feature that makes hold'em so exciting is the fact that every other player also gets to use those same five board cards to make his hand. Sometimes you will have to use both cards in your hand to make a poker hand and sometimes you will only need one card in your hand. Less often, the highest possible hand will be the five cards on the board and that will be your poker hand. That's called *playing the board*.

If your hole cards are A♦ K♣ and the board is 10♠ J♥ Q♠ 7♦ 3♥, then you have an ace-high straight.

YOU

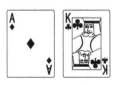

BOARD

If your hole cards are A♦ K♣ and the board is J♦ 9♦ 8♣ 5♦ 2♦, then you have an ace-high diamond flush.

YOU

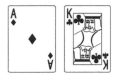

BOARD

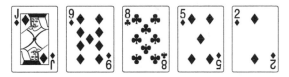

If your hole cards are A♦ K♣ and the board is A♠ A♥ K♠ 8♣ 5♥, then you have a full house: aces full of kings.

YOU

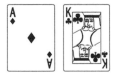

BOARD

I thought that was aces over kings?

No, that's a common misconception. They even get it wrong on television sometimes. Aces full means that you have a full house and your three of a kind is the aces. Aces over means that you have two pair and your highest pair is the aces.

If your hole cards are A♦ K♣ and the board is Q♥ 9♣ K♦ 5♠ 5♥, then your hand is two pair: kings and fives with an ace kicker.

Kicker? What's that?

Every poker hand must consist of exactly five cards. That's a universal rule that applies to all forms of poker and to all poker games. A kicker is the fourth or fifth card in your poker hand that is not part of the combination that forms one pair, two pair or trips. If you have A-K and your opponent has K-J and the board is K-9-7-4-3, then you win because you have a pair of kings with an ace kicker and he has a pair of kings with a jack kicker.

If your hand is K♣ K♠ and the board is 9♠ 8♦ 7♥ 6♣ 5♠, then your hand is not a pair of kings. It's a 9-high straight and if you call the last bet and turn your hand face up, you will split the pot with any other player whose best hand is the board as well. Notice, however, that any player holding a 10 in his hand will have a 10-high straight and will beat you. Also notice that the best possible hand here is to be holding J-10 to make an unbeatable jack-high straight. That's the *nuts*.

The nuts?

Yes, that's the term used in flop and community card games to designate the very best possible hand at any stage of the game, given the cards on the board. That's one of the best features of hold'em: You always know what it takes to win or tie the hand.

PLAYING IN A PUBLIC CARDROOM

Okay, I think I know enough about how to play Texas hold'em to give it a try in a public cardroom. What do I need to know to get ready?

Keep in mind that poker is a game where you're betting that you know what you're doing. In this case, you must realize that you're a beginner and the players you'll be playing against are going to be better players than you are right now.

Okay, how do I put that knowledge into action?

You should look for the lowest limit hold'em game that you think you'd be comfortable in. If you live in Las Vegas, you can find several good $1/$2, $2/$4 or $1-$4 spread-limit games around town. These are excellent games for beginning players. You will be playing against mostly other beginners for small stakes and be able to gain a lot of good experience with minimal risk to your bankroll. And, if you follow the rest of the advice in this book, you'll probably be a winner and be able to move up to higher stakes later.

Is that how you started out in hold'em?
Oh, no. I played my first games of Texas hold'em in the Stardust poker room at the $10/$20 tables. This was back in the 1980s and my opponents were nice folks like Cissy Bottoms and Ted Forrest. I didn't know any better and I didn't have anyone teaching me. I took my lessons at the table where you have to either learn to play better or go broke. I did both.

What else should I know?
You should realize that a poker session does not consist of just one game. You may end up playing for a long time, for hours on end, and you might juggle other commitments to make more time for poker. For that reason, you should try to go alone, take your own car, have an open-ended quitting time, and be flexible. Sometimes a game is just too good and profitable to leave and sometime it's just too bad to leave.

You should bring with you whatever items you would ordinarily need in the course of a day out. Bring your prescription medication, aspirin, cigarettes and sweater if you think you'll be there more than a few hours. Once you arrive in a poker room new to you, you need to familiarize yourself with the house rules.

House rules? I thought poker was pretty much the same everywhere.
It mostly is, but there are a lot of questions about player conduct that have to be addressed ahead of time. The

poker room has done this by posting their house rules. A sample list of house rules might look like this:

HOUSE RULES

1. All games are table stakes.

2. English only may be spoken during the play of a hand.

3. Check and raise is allowed.

4. A maximum of three (or four or five) raises are allowed.

5. One player per hand.

6. No string bets allowed.

7. No eating at the table.

8. This is a no-smoking poker room.

9. The decision of the floorperson is final.

Okay, I just took my seat in my first hold'em game in a public cardroom. What else should I know?
You should decide how much to buy in for. I recommend you make it $100 for a $1/$2 game and $200 for a $2/$4 game. This is enough to allow you to play the game without having to worry about your bankroll. You'll be able to lose a few hands (which happens to all of us) and still be able to stay in the game to give yourself a chance to win a few hands to get your money back.

A very good-looking almost-dressed woman just asked me if I wanted a cocktail. What should I do?

That was the cocktail waitress. She will bring you all the alcohol and other drinks that you want from the bar for free as long as you're playing in the poker game. You should not drink alcohol since you're playing a game of skill. That would not be a good thing. Also, remember you might have to drive home. If you have to drink, wait until you get home. You can get water, coffee and juice for free. Just remember that the cocktail waitress works for tips.

What happens if I have to go to the restroom or take a short break?

It helps the dealer and everyone else at the table if you can stay at the table when it's your big and small blind. That's so you don't miss a blind and the dealer does not have to advance the button and require three blinds when you return. If you're going to be gone long enough to miss exactly one hand, then you should make it the hand right before you're due to have the big blind. If you're going to miss two hands then you should wait until it is your turn in the big blind to leave. Then you will miss both the big and the small blinds and when you return, you will be in late position when you post your missed blinds. Late position and already in! That's great.

The dealer seems to be very concerned about how I place my chips when I bet. What's going on?

Dealers vary in how they like to run the game. Some dealers like to make change for each individual player as it is each player's turn to act. Other dealers like to collect all the bets and then return your change after the betting and raising is complete. They are also making sure that you don't throw an indeterminate number of chips into the pot, thereby making it impossible to tell how much you called with. This is called *splashing the pot* and it is not allowed.

What is poker etiquette?
It refers to how you should conduct yourself during the game. Good etiquette requires that you don't criticize the way another player plays his hand, that you don't get involved in arguments or disputes over the game unless you're in the hand in question, and that you don't needlessly "Hollywood."

Hollywood. I know that's where they make movies, but how's that related to my poker game?
Hollywooding means that you don't take a very long time to make a decision or make a play that you knew from the beginning that you were going to make anyway. In other words, don't delay on purpose when it's your turn to act just for the attention. On those rare occasions when you do need some extra time to act, the dealer and the players will usually allow you all the time you need because they know you'll be acting in good faith.

Anything else?
Yes. It's both polite and considerate if you're always ready to act when it's your turn.

If there had to be one last thing I had to know, what would that be?
Remember that even though you're acting in your own best interests against the other players, that it is a game that requires everyone's attention to keep running smoothly. If a player turns his cards face up at the end of the hand and the dealer misreads it, or is about to award the pot to the wrong player, you are allowed to speak up to help remedy the situation. The truth is whatever it is, and the actual winner is determined by the cards, even if there was some confusion over the hand.

3.
HAND SELECTION

It's been said that the biggest winner in any poker game is the player who plays the fewest hands. I've been playing poker for more than twenty-five years and I can tell you that it's mostly true. Everyone is going to be dealt their fair share of winning hands, but the trick is to not give your winnings back on losing hands in between those winning hands. Doyle Brunson said, "It's not the hands you play, but the hands you don't play that will determine if you're a winner."

I briefly covered the subject of hand selection in my first book in this series, *Ken Warren Teaches Texas Hold'em.* Since then, I've received dozens of email requests for more examples of which hands to play, more detailed explanations of why to play certain hands, and more insight into the thinking process that goes into hand selection. I'm going to answer those questions here.

Keep in mind that the first consideration in hand selection is the very nature of the game itself. The essence of all poker games is the fact that high cards and high hands beat lower cards and lower hands. This does not mean that two higher cards are always automatically good while two lower cards are instantly bad.

PREFLOP STRATEGY
This is one aspect of hold'em that is a little more cut-and-dried than other facets of the game. It's safe to follow

some specific guidelines and principles when deciding whether, how, and why to play your hand before the flop. The fact that there has been very little action so far in the game means that you don't have to analyze countless decisions by the other players. The availability of information is limited, which makes your decisions easier and more straightforward.

Well then, how do I know which hands to play?
Luckily, this is a fairly easy question to answer. Millions of poker players have played billions of poker hands over the years. Their collective wisdom taught them that certain beginning hands were vastly more profitable than others, and that many other hands are certain losers in the overall long-term.

What did they find out?
Just due to the very nature of poker, higher cards are almost always more profitable than lower cards.

What do you mean by "almost always"?
There are exceptions. Some lower ranking hands can be very profitable under the right circumstances.

What does that mean?
It means that hands that might be 3 to 1 or 4 to 1 underdogs can win money in the long run if there's enough money in the pot to overcome those odds.

How do you overcome odds? Is that possible?

Look at it this way: Assume you are holding a hand like 8♣ 7♣, which is about a 3 to 1 underdog in a multiway hold'em game. You play it one time and lose $12. Then you lose two more times with it for a total loss of $36. These three losses are represented by the "3" in the 3 to 1 equation. Then you play it a fourth time while investing another $12 and this time you win the hand. You've invested $48 in the hands and if there's more than $48 in the one pot you've won, then you're an overall winner in the long term with that hand. You've overcome the odds.

How do I put this information to use?

You have to learn when to play that hand so that you have a good chance to win a big pot if you do win the hand.

When *do* I play that hand and hands like it?

Ideally, when you're in late position and there's less chance of a raise after you limp in. You also need to have a lot of players already in the pot ahead of you. This is so that when you connect with those cards, a lot of players will put money into a pot that you're going to win. As you can see, you need a lot of money in the pot to make up for the times you played the hand and lost.

Anything else?

Yes. Would you believe that you can win the hand with those cards and still have done the wrong thing?

How can that be? Isn't a win a win? How can you win and still be a loser?

Interesting question. This is one of those things that makes poker appear to be easy to play when it really is not. Not all wins and losses are equal. Six losing hands followed by six winning hands does not mean you're even. Obviously, in the above example, if you lose $36 on three hands but don't win back that $36 on your one winning hand, then you're a loser with that hand in the long run. You want to avoid having a negative expectation.

What is a negative expectation?

Basically, it's the total amount of money you expect to win or lose on a particular hand if the hand is played over the long run.

What is a positive expectation?

It's when your expected wins add up to more than your losses for each particular, unique hand you play.

What else do we know about hand selection?

Thanks to the computer revolution, we can say with a great deal of certainty when you should play certain hands in which positions and why.

Why is that?

It's because a computer allows us to compress time and keep perfectly accurate records. In the old days, it might take a player as long as twenty years to gain enough experience and raw data to draw conclusions about what works and what doesn't. A computer can play the same hands one million times in one minute. Every hand can be analyzed from every position under every circumstance by a computer. Modern-day students of poker can now start their poker educations at the point where older players took decades to get to.

What do I need to know about hand selection?
I'm going to teach you a method of choosing which hands you're going to play before the flop in Texas hold'em. These hands are proven winners in the long run. If you stick to playing just the hands in the following list, you will be able to stay out of trouble and not lose your entire bankroll while you're learning the other aspects of the game. I'm going to teach you how to play three types of starting hands. Playing these hands correctly will allow you to take advantage of one the best key features of Texas hold'em over other poker games.

What is the best key feature of Texas hold'em?
It's the fact that if you can limp in before the flop for just one small bet and 71 percent of your hand for the least possible investment. No other poker games except pineapple and Omaha offer you a risk-to-reward ratio like that. This brings us to another important winning concept.

What is that new winning concept?
It's the idea that, in all forms of poker, you should usually put as little money in the pot as possible until you can clearly see that you can win the hand (or have a

positive expectation based on the risk-to-reward ratio of hitting a winning hand), or you should fold. Minimize your losses — maximize your wins.

If you hold A♥ Q♦ and the flop is Q♠ 9♥ 6♦, then there are only two more cards left to be seen. You don't have to wait to see those cards one at a time, as you would in stud games, which have a betting round after every card is received.

What are pineapple and Omaha?
They are flop games like hold'em and with only one difference: the number of cards you're dealt before the flop. You get three private cards in pineapple and four in Omaha.

What are those three types of good Texas hold'em starting hands?
1. The first type is pocket pairs
Anytime your first two hole cards are a pair, you will usually want to either raise, call, or sometimes fold with those pairs. I'll be more specific in a little bit.

2. The second type of hand is suited aces
That means your hand is playable if you have an ace and another card that is the same suit as your ace.

3. The third type of hand is called a 20 or 21 hand
Using the blackjack system of adding up the value of cards, aces are worth 11 points, face cards are worth 10 points and the other cards are worth their pip value.

What is a pip?

It's the number of spades, diamonds, hearts, and clubs on the cards numbered 2 through 9. The 5♦ has five pips, the 8♣ has eight pips and so on. An ace has only one pip. Prior to about 1876, playing cards had pips only, and no numbers (called an *index*) on them.

Which blackjack hands do I play?

Any two cards that add up to 20 or 21. An ace and a face card, an ace and a 9 and two face cards are the only hands in this category. While we're on the subject of adding up the value of cards, be sure to observe the Rule of 13.

What is the Rule of 13?

It means you should never play any two cards that add up to 13, with the single exception of an ace and a deuce of the same suit (A♣ 2♣, A♠ 2♠, A♥ 2♥ and A♦ 2♦). That means you cannot play these hands: K-3, Q-3, J-3, 10-3, 9-4, 8-5, or 7-6. It's one of the few rules in poker than you can blindly follow without having to worry that you might be missing profits. Don't worry about it.

Where do we start? I need you to give me specific advice for every hand

Let's start with the biggest, the best and the most profitable. Pocket aces is the best hand you can get to begin a hold'em game. If the hand were over right there, you'd win every time. There is no better hand.

How do I play pocket aces before the flop?

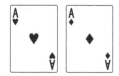

It depends on your position at the table relative to the big blind, how many players have already acted on their hands, how many players have yet to act, and what you think the other players might be holding.

Okay, let's say I'm first after the big blind

Pocket aces play best and win more often against fewer players rather than more. So you should raise the big blind to drive out the other players. If a player does call, then you have a better idea of what he might have because he thought it was worth calling a raise with. You are a huge favorite over any other player calling with a pocket pair. If you are raised, you should always reraise. This will help drive out other players, help isolate the other raiser and get more money into a pot that you expect to win most of the time. You should be willing to reraise the maximum number of times allowed since you're going to win with this hand more than any other. You should usually raise before the flop with pocket aces no matter what your position is because it usually reduces the field while increasing the size of the pot.

You said, "usually"

Yes. Sometimes you might want to just call for several reasons. The first is that you might want to disguise the strength of your hand. You might be waiting until the turn, when the bets double, to put in a raise. Or, you might be playing second hand low.

What is second hand low?
It's when you just call with the best hand hoping that someone behind you will raise so that you can reraise them. This traps them for an extra bet when they have the worst hand.

You should usually raise on the button for a reason that doesn't have anything to do with the strength of your hand.

What can that reason possibly be?
When you raise from late position before the flop, you indicate strength. Many times, everyone will check to the raiser on the flop because they assume you'll bet because you raised earlier. When they check to you, you can also check if you don't like the flop. Your preflop raise chilled the action on the flop and now you get to see the turn card for free. Your preflop raise bought you a free card. Sometimes, everyone will check again on the turn, assuming that *now* you'll bet. You can check right behind them and see the river card for free. One raise before the flop enabled you to see the entire hand for free.

Just a little tip: If you raise preflop with pocket aces and lose the hand, the winner is more likely to be on your immediate right than on your left.

Why is that?

Well, the players on your left called your raise. This means they have better than average hands and are more likely to have pocket pairs and not drawing hands. Your pocket aces will always be a big favorite over those pairs, no matter what they are. Pocket kings is no more a favorite over you than pocket deuces. They both have to improve to beat you. The player on your right, however, could have called with anything, and statistically speaking, he likely has a drawing hand if he didn't raise. He's in for one bet, you're trapped for another, but he will usually have a hand that is not dominated by pocket aces. He will very often be drawing with live cards, and that's what will more frequently beat your pocket aces.

How do I play the other pocket pairs before the flop?

This is one of two hands that I *always* raise with before the flop. What's the other hand, you ask? Read on. I can't remember the last time I limped in with pocket kings. The reason is that I don't like to get beat by someone holding A♣ 6♥ when they get an ace on the flop. Give the players holding aces with garbage kickers a reason to fold before the flop. You'll get an ace on the flop about 22 percent of the time. There are only four of them in the deck. Only one or two of them, on average, will be dealt out before the flop. If you can get a player to fold his ace before the flop, then the presence of an ace on the flop is less of a threat to you. If you raise preflop and then bet on the flop when no ace comes, a player holding A♠ 8♦ will probably throw his hand away. That way, an ace on the turn or river probably won't kill your pair of kings.

If you're in the big or small blind, you are usually not going to force anyone who's already called to fold if you raise. What will usually happen is that your raise will just build the pot and you might even get a reraise from one of the players who originally just called.

Just a little tip: If you have pocket kings and you don't want players to call your raise, it helps just a little bit if you can raise immediately without giving them much time to think about their hands. That's because the longer a player has to look at his hand before acting on it, the longer he has to talk himself into looking for reasons to call. Make him decide to muck the hand before he can fall in love with it.

I will raise preflop with this hand if I think it will cause other players to fold. That's so that if an ace or king comes on the flop, it might not pair up one of my opponents. Otherwise, I like to limp in with it and hope to flop a set. I'll then have a well disguised strong hand.

If it's raised, I will usually reraise for the other reasons: I have a big hand that figures to win more than its fair share in the long run and I don't mind building a pot. You will get one or more aces or kings on the flop 41 percent of the time.

I almost never raise before the flop with this hand unless I'm on the button and almost everybody's in the pot. I'll then raise to build a huge pot, hoping to flop a set. If I hit—great. If I miss—it's cost me only one extra small bet and I can let the hand go if need be. You will flop overcards without making a set 47 percent of the time. For that reason, I like to see the flop as cheaply as possible. The other time I raise with pocket jacks is if no one has entered the pot and I feel like I can steal the blinds or at least make them check to me on the flop.

This is definitely a vulnerable hand. Almost any kind of flop can represent a real threat to this pocket pair. You almost have to flop either a set or a 7-8-9 or 8-9-J to have a hand. And even then, you can still be beat. Top professional hold'em players say that pocket tens is one of the most difficult hands to play preflop.

Other Pocket Pairs:

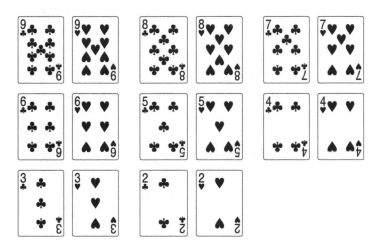

I put all of these pocket pairs in the same category because they all have the same problems, drawbacks, potential for loss, and potential for winnings. I don't get one bit more excited when I look down and see 9♣ 9♥ than I do when I see 2♣ 2♥. You have to flop a set to win a big pot with these hands. If you win without flopping a set, the pot will usually be small.

Is there anything that expert hold'em players know about small pocket pairs that beginners don't know?
Yes, and it's simply the fact that you don't have to play the hand at all if you don't want to. There's no law that says you must call before the flop when you hold a pocket pair. Under some very specific and extreme

circumstances, this also applies to big pocket pairs including jack, queens and even kings.

I admit I'm weak. I like to play hands that I know I shouldn't sometimes. Can you help me with that?
Yes. There is an exercise that you can perform that helps you with not playing too many hands. And that is to simply decide which hands you're going to play and decide to play them *ahead* of time. This is called having a game plan. What you do is look at your first card when you get it. Let's say it's the 7♣ and you've decided that you're going to play only pocket pairs and suited aces. This card obviously can't be combined with any other card to add up to 20 or 21, so that's not a factor here. You tell yourself, "My next card has be either another 7, the 6♣, the 8♣ or the A♣." Do this before you get your second card. Then you look at the second card, and if it's not one of the cards you named, then you should instantly throw the hand away. Don't hesitate and don't talk yourself into breaking your rule.

There's a few hands that I just *love* to play and I really don't want to stop playing them. Is there anything I can do to limit my losses?
Yes. You can put yourself in the best possible position and give yourself the best possible chance to win with these hands. Don't play these hands all the time under all circumstances. You're going to have to compromise. Play them only when you're in very late position, only when there are a lot of other players in the pot, and if possible, in late position with a lot of players. This is

about the best you can do. If you can limp in for only one small bet and then fold if you miss the flop, that might be profitable. If you're last to act, you can fold if you're obviously beat, or you can raise and get in an extra bet if you hit the flop.

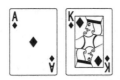

This is the other hand that I always raise preflop with. I really like this hand for a lot of good reasons. This is what you'll get on the flop with A-K suited:

FLOP PROBABILITIES WITH A-K SUITED

28.960%	One ace or king
2.021%	An ace and a king
.837%	Flopped flush
.005%	Flopped royal flush
1.300%	Two more aces or kings
10.944%	Two more of your suit
7.930%	Four to a straight
.092%	Full house
52.089%	**TOTAL**

When you hold A-K suited, you will flop a good hand or a good draw an incredible 53 percent of the time. That's 1 to 1 odds on the draw when the pot odds are often 6 to 1 or even 9 to 1. This is a hugely profitable situation and it's one of the best bets in hold'em. Since you will flop a lot of nut flush and straight draw hands, many of the pots you win with this hand will be very big. You also have the advantage of winning all showdowns when everyone misses their draws.

The statistics for these hands are nearly identical as for the above A-K suited. They are all royal flush cards and big winners in the long run.

Any suited hand with an ace in it is usually playable to see the flop, but you do have to be more careful as your kicker gets smaller and smaller. If you start with one of these hands, you'll finish with a flush only about one time in thirty. It's about 11 to 1 against flopping two more cards of your suit and it's only 35 percent that you'll make the flush after that.

You should usually play these hands as if they're not suited until you see the flop. Their value before the flop is not that much greater than their unsuited counterparts, but once you make a flush, the hand has fantastic value because it will be the nut flush and usually the nut hand. You'll win big pots and be able to get in extra bets with confidence.

Do you have any preflop secrets you're willing to share with us?

Okay, just this one: I really like all combinations of royal flush cards. From A♥ K♥ down through J♥ 10♥. It's because I know from my statistical research that they are all big winners in the long run. However, the length of time that it takes a hand to show a profit and exactly what that profit is varies with the hand.

I will almost always raise and reraise before the flop with these hands in late position because I know that it's the right thing to do in the long run. I don't expect immediate, daily guarantees of a profit with these hands, but I know it will come over time. These are speculative, drawing hands, but they're good ones.

And now we take a look at the big unsuited hands.

I normally do not raise before the flop with A-K unsuited. It seems that I make the most money with this hand when I limp in and muck it if I miss the flop. I only invest a lot of money in the hand after the flop when I have much more information than I did before the flop. Also, your hand will be disguised if you limp in and hit the flop.

Do you have any tips for playing big slick after the flop?
You normally don't want to slowplay this hand, but I will sometimes do that when I have A-K and I flop an

ace. If the flop is A♦ 8♥ 3♠ and I'm sure my opponent also has an ace, I'll sometimes check and call on the flop and check-raise on the turn. You make more money this way if you know your opponent. You also risk giving a free card that might beat you, but that event is mitigated by two facts: Your opponent was going to call if you bet and the card that beats you was coming whether you check or bet.

Another time you might check with A-K when an ace flops is when you know your opponent does not have an ace or won't call if you bet. Give him a chance to represent an ace and try to steal a pot from you now and then. It's profitable.

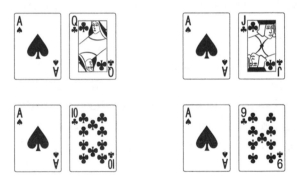

When you play a hand with an ace in it, it's because you're looking to flop an ace and win the hand. For that to happen, you need your kicker to be good. And for that reason, you have a weak, vulnerable and unprofitable hand if you play an ace with a kicker weaker than a 9.

These hands can all make the nut ace-high straight. They can also make a good two-pair hand that wins a lot of pots. You should see the flop as cheaply as possible with these hands unless you're raising to steal the blinds.

Do you have an overall philosophy about preflop play?
Yes, I do. And that is, I don't like to play in raised pots unless I'm the raiser. I understand that you can't win every hand and the nature of normal card distribution means that every hand can have a different winner than the hand before. If someone else raises before the flop, then that tells me that he has a much better hand than average and therefore, he has a much better chance of ending up the winner. I've learned to stay out of his way and let him win that hand. I'll wait for a hand to play where *I* can be the raiser. I act like we have an agreement to take turns winning hands and the preflop raise tells whose turn it is. It's a level of patience that comes with age, experience, and a desire to be a winner. You can't win every hand, but you can let the cards help you decide which hands you might win with.

Speaking of not winning every hand, what's the most consecutive number of hands that you've won?
In twenty-five years of playing, I've won only seven consecutive hands. It was at the old Showboat poker room in Las Vegas in 1988.

What about these in-the-middle-hands you mentioned earlier?
There's a group of hands that are not high, but not low hands either. It seems that a lot of players just love any two cards between a jack and a 5 and they play them all the time. Especially hands like Q-8, J-8, 10-7, 10-6, 9-8, 9-7 and 8-6.

What's wrong with these hands?
On the one hand, they can win some big pots. If you hold medium-strength cards and you get a flop to match, you can make a straight and win a big pot. But so can everyone else who plays these cards. When you miss your straight draw, or make a pair that's no good, you lose to the player holding higher cards than what you've got.

On the other hand, when you win with these hands, it's just a temporary win.

Why is it just a temporary win?
It's because all of the players in your game who play these types of hands (and there are a lot of them) will take turns winning the hand when the board cooperates with middle-strength cards. These players, in effect, just

end up passing that one big pot around to each other during the course of the game while the pot gets raked every time and then stolen from them by a better player playing better cards.

What is a trouble hand?

It's a hand that looks very good but actually does not perform that well. Most players never realize it because the hand *looks* so good. K-Q under the gun is a trouble hand. Players who call after you are often able to beat you. If you flop a king or a queen, you're in trouble against A-K and A-Q hands as well as aces and kings. Aces with small kickers are also trouble hands. The worst thing that can happen to you is to flop another ace and have a bettor or caller.

Do you have any other preflop advice?

Yes. I think it's very important that you put a lot of effort into selecting good hands to play.

4.
LOW-LIMIT CONCEPTS AND STRATEGY

STEPPING DOWN TO REFRESH IDEAS

If you're a higher limit player, I think it might be a good idea for you to seek out a low-limit game, just for the experience. You always hear about players being urged to occasionally take a chance in a higher limit game than what they're used to, but you don't hear about players being urged to play in a lower limit game. A sudden streak of bad luck might force you to step down in limit. Why not give it a try because you want to, and not because you have to?

There are benefits to this. First of all, it will refresh your memory. You'll see lots of other players' mistakes and obvious situations unfold. You'll be able to predict the future and see mistakes made that you'd never make. It will also boost your confidence, reinforce your good habits, and to top it off, you might have a bit of fun and learn something. And, oh—you might win some money. The players in these games typically play very badly, which means that they will almost always call when they should fold. They will play every hand, chase every draw, and try to catch every bluff on the river. It seems that there are many ways to win a hand of poker, but the only one that you can use against these players is to have the best hand at the river.

When you play these games, you will often have big fluctuations in your stacks and you will seem to have no control at all over your cards and your opponents. Be patient. It takes a long time to beat bad players. Don't go on tilt when someone puts a bad beat on you. The fact is, if you could have seen their cards during the play of the hand, you'd have wanted them to play anyway. Don't give up — the cards will average out in the long run. Your job is to still be in the game when that happens.

You can only win what the circumstances will give you in a game like this. You can't bully your way to a win. You usually can't bluff. It's difficult to represent a hand because your opponents aren't sophisticated enough to read your hands. All they know is what their cards are and what the flop is. And on the other hand, it seems that there's always one or two other players in the game who are knowledgeable, studious, careful and are trying to play the right way. They may not always be great players, but they're still better than most of the other players in the game.

Since you're going to do this for practice, I recommend you buy in for only $40. That's so you can put on the pressure to win early in the game, and so you have practice nursing that small bankroll like your life depends on it. Make every decision one that will win you the pot. Play only premium hands. Take advantage of your position. Do everything you can to keep from busting out and having to rebuy.

The concept of playing your hand according to what position you're in is a fairly advanced idea in poker. That's why you won't see much respect for position in a $2/$4 game. Players will play any hand from any seat and they won't make adjustments (play tighter) as their position relative to the dealer gets worse. They don't understand the idea of protecting big hands before the flop.

That means that you can limp in from early position with weaker hands than usual because you won't be punished by a better hand calling from your left. Your call induces other calls and this gives you better implied odds. It starts to become correct to play the hand past the flop and on to the river before the preflop action is over. Big pots before the flop means more players taking more chances all the way to the end.

STRATEGY CONSIDERATIONS

You need a long-term strategy for a game like this. You should bet for value, and check and check-raise when it's the right thing to do. Make percentage calls on the river, look out for frequent bluffers and know the odds. Most of all, be patient. Don't let the frequent bad beat nature of the game get to you. That's what makes it profitable in the long run.

A big, costly mistake that's made by someone almost every hand is calling with two big cards when they totally miss the flop. If you have K♥ Q♦ and the flop is 8♠ 5♦ 3♣, you will have to muck your hand if there's a bet. But that won't happen in this game. A player holding two big cards will usually call all the way hoping to snag a king or a queen on the turn or river. And guess what? They occasionally get one and win the hand. This is especially true if they hold A♥ K♦.

Players holding medium pocket pairs will almost always call the flop, regardless if there are overcards that obviously beat them. If the flop is 10♠ J♠ K♥, someone holding 7♠ 7♦ will still call you, even if they think they are temporarily behind.

One of the blinds will sometimes check-raise. It usually means he has the nuts or near-nuts at this point or he is on a big draw. If the flop is 8♠ 7♠ 5♦, he will either have a straight flush draw, a made straight, or perhaps a set. What he will not have is top pair with a good kicker.

If the board is A♦ 9♦ 8♣ 7♦ 6♦, you will often see one player with a small diamond bet the hand. You will also see players bet with the 10-high straight and others with the ignorant end of the straight holding a 5. In a higher limit game, the only betting that will take place is by someone holding the K♦ or the Q♦.

Whenever the turn and river cards come perfect-perfect to make a possible straight or flush, you have to consider it to be a real threat. Players who have three-card straights and flushes will often call to "see just one more card" in an effort to pick up a four-straight or a four-flush. And then, after getting that card on the turn, they have a reasonable draw to see the river card. You make money from them in this situation because they will miss the draw about 80 percent of the time on the turn. You win those extra bets in the pot when they have to fold on the river.

When the board presents a possible straight draw — say the flop is J♠ 9♦ 7♥ — there is a situation that often occurs that makes the hand easy to read. And that is when the turn and river cards are both 8-8 or 10-10. That's because a player holding A♠ 10♦ or A♠ 8♦ will have flopped a gutshot straight draw and will almost always take one off to try to make the straight. You can usually be sure that a player originally on a straight draw now has trips, and sometimes, a full house.

Your profit in these low-limit games comes from two main sources:

1. Players who play so loose that they put money in the pot when they have no reasonable chance to win.

2. The fact that the games gets looser and wilder as it goes on.

What I mean is that, in the first hour or two of a game, you might win $14 in an average pot with a hand like A♠ J♥. Hours later in the same game, you might win a $45 pot with those same hole cards, the same flop, turn and river as you had earlier. You don't win more money by playing more hands; you win more money because the players put more money in the pot on the hands you do play.

RAISING CONCEPTS

It's a generally accepted truth that there are five main reasons to raise in poker, and hold'em in particular. Those reasons are:

1. To get players to fold.

2. To get them to check to you on the next betting round. This is known as getting a free card, even though that's not technically true.

3. To gain information.

4. To get value (extract money from losing hands) for your hand.

5. To bluff or semi-bluff.

If you look at this list of reasons to raise, and you think about your typical low-limit game, you just might break out in laughter. You can easily see how these reasons to raise almost don't work in a low-limit game.

Who's going to fold just because you raised before the flop? It will usually only be the player who was going to fold anyway and it didn't matter to him that you raised. He wasn't going to call one bet, let alone two bets anyway. Players who were going to call one bet will usually go ahead and call two bets to see the flop.

If you raised to make the other players check into you on the next betting round, then good luck. Most low-limit players aren't sophisticated enough to know that your raise means that they're already behind and they're still behind after the flop. They will bet into you if they have anything at all, not knowing that it's the wrong thing to do.

Raising to gain information is a vastly overrated move in low limit. When you raise to gain information, you are, in effect, asking a question. Your opponents' response to your raise is the answer to that question. The problem is that there's too much room for ambiguity and misunderstanding of the action. Does he even know that your raise is asking a question about his hand? Does he know how to disguise his answer? Is he answering the right question? Are you getting an answer to the question you asked, or is he unwittingly answering a different question?

And finally, what is your degree of confidence? Are you 100 percent sure that his calling your raise tells you exactly what you want to know? Could you have gotten the same information without raising? How much more are you going to earn or save because of your raise? Would it have been cheaper and just as effective to not raise?

I can tell you that if you're an average, beginning player (and be honest with yourself because this advice is worth money to you), a raise used solely to gain information before the flop or on the flop is usually not worth the investment. It's because of all the problems mentioned above and the fact that you're usually overpaying for information that you can't use anyway. Save your money and raise for other reasons if you can see the logic in this.

Raising to get value from your hand is the best reason of all to raise at any time of the game. You should raise any time you're the favorite to win the hand. The reason comes from the very definition of what a favorite is. It means that the player who is ahead early in the game starts out with a better than average chance of being the winner at the end of the game. In a situation like that, you'd rather play for more money than less. Raise. They will call you; it's what makes them the bad players that they are.

Raising to bluff is an advanced move not known to the average low-limit player. It is rarely successful. It's a move that has its best results only in higher limit games and in no-limit games. It's not really part of the low-limit game.

When you go back and look at the list of reasons to raise, you can see that it's difficult to accomplish the intended goal of the raise. And that's due to the fact that low-limit players aren't yet knowledgeable enough to respect a raise.

The closing advice on raising is this: Raise when you have the best hand before the flop and on the flop; and raise on the turn and the river only when you know weaker hands will pay you off. Otherwise, just usually call.

A LEARNING EXERCISE: FOCUS ON ONE PLAYER

If you're a higher limit player and you're playing $2/$4 just for the fun of it, there's a few things you can do to add to the fun, if you're willing. It will enable you to try a few tricks without worrying about losing a large amount of money.

Not all the players in a low limit game are horrible. Some of them are reasonably good and try to play correctly, as far as they know. You can pick the best player at your table and adjust your game just for him. Watch his every move. Keep track of how many hands he plays. What's the worst hands he'll play in certain positions? Does he play every ace? Does he play low cards? Does he always call in the small blind? Can you read his hands? If so, can you figure out when to bluff or raise him out of a pot? Focus on just this one player. If you're both in a hand with other players, you can use him as a barometer for figuring out those players. If he's a regular in that game and you're the newcomer, let him be the leader when playing against the other players. After all, he knows them better than you do. This will give you some practice studying other players without risking a big buy-in.

Here's an extension of the above advice that will help you win an extra pot or two. Pick one player to watch only on the river. Look to see what hands he will bet and raise with relative to the board. How close to the nuts does he have to have to feel confident about a bet for value on the river? Will top pair with top kicker do it? The secret here is to figure out the worst hand that he'll bet for value, on average. Once you figure that out, you can pick a spot to raise him on the river when there's a board that you think will make him fold. Try to confidently represent a better hand and if you've timed it right, he will fold. You only need to win one or two pots like this per session to show a huge profit—and don't ever show your hand if you don't have to.

AN EXERCISE IN THE POWER OF POSITION

Legendary poker player Doyle Brunson once said that he could play and win with no cards at all whenever he was in late position or on the button. Of course, he was talking about no-limit, which makes it a heck of lot easier to win a hand when you can bet a lot of money.

Doyle's statement about the power of position led me to try an exercise that proved to be both instructional and profitable. Whenever I'm in a low-limit game and I see that my first hole card is an ace or a king, I will see if I can win the hand just based on my late position in the game. I will not look at my other card and when it's my turn to act, I will raise and reraise before the flop. I'll push the hand all the way through and I'll bet at the end. That's because I know, both statistically speaking and from experience, that an uncalled bet on the river is the most common winning hand in hold'em.

Not knowing my other hole card helps emphasize the fact that I have to win based on position. I force myself to try to do that by betting hands that I would not otherwise bet. What I've learned is that it works! I've won many games with hands that I would not have ordinarily won with because I would not have bet my cards. When I bet based on my position, I win often enough to show a big profit. This has really taught me the value of position. And besides, it's really fun when I get called and have to expose my second hole card when I haven't even seen it yet myself. The only time I look at it is when I'm raised on the river and I'm the last to act. In that case, I have everything to gain and nothing to lose by looking.

This exercise—which I try only in the low-limit game—has been very valuable to me. It's taught me the value of position and has given me the confidence to bet on the river more often in the higher limit games.

IMPROVING YOUR PLAY

If you're a beginning hold'em player, but you're astute enough to read this and other poker books, then you probably realize that hold'em is a tough game to learn to play perfectly. You undoubtedly know that you don't know it all yet. I can help you with that. All you need is a little bit of organization and thought on the subject. You know that when you play, there are parts of the game that you don't fully understand or that you know you're not good at. Perhaps you have some bad habits and you're aware of that fact. That's good. Self-awareness is the beginning of learning and advancement.

All you have to do is make a few quick notes to yourself when you think of something you can work on.

- Do you call too much?

- Do you play too many hands?

- See too many flops?

- Call when you know you're beat?

- Play too tight?

- Fold too early?

- Don't bluff?

- Don't try to read other player's hands?

And so on. All you have to do is make a list of these nagging thoughts as they come to mind and then put them in order, with the worst one at the top of the list. And then, all you do is concentrate and work on that one item. Talk out loud to yourself. Discuss it with fellow poker players. Look for a poker book that addresses your problem, read poker magazines, or look up relevant information online.

The point is to actively do something about it. Once you identify, isolate and address the problem, you'll be surprised to see how easy it is to manage from there.

There's a joke from college management courses that will help you see the point:

Question: How do you eat an elephant?

Answer: One bite at a time.

This will help you get into the habit of thinking about poker. Once you've solved the problem at the top of your list, then go to work on the next biggest problem. You'll find that as you go through this process and become a better player, the problems will get smaller, easier to solve, and the game will be more fun. That's because it's more fun when you win.

When you're in a hand, one of the most important factors in determining your chances of winning the hand is, obviously, your cards. But there's another factor that's just as important, if not more important. And that is how many players are in the hand with you. Obviously, the fewer the players there are in the hand, the better your odds are to win the hand. And there will be fewer players at the end that you will have to bet and bluff through.

There's another exercise you can perform that will help highlight this one aspect of the game. It's simple: Always raise before the flop if you're going to play a hand and you're the first one in after the blinds. Before the flop is the best time to get players to fold. That's because there's nothing in the pot to fight for and your raise means that they have to have a playable hand to call with.

You will often cause everyone to fold and the blinds will call because they already have one bet in the pot. This puts you in a great position—last with a playable hand against the blinds. This is a very profitable situation to be in. You can then begin to bet just because you're in last position, as you learned in the previous exercise, above. The pots will be smaller, but you will win more often.

There's still another thing you can do while playing a low-limit game that will make it more fun and more profitable for you. And that is to play the overs. *Playing the overs* is the term for playing at a higher limit when only certain players are in the hand. If you're in a $2/$4 game then the most you can bet is $4 on the river. However, if you are an overs player and the only other player or players left in the game at the beginning of the betting round are also overs players, then you can bet an amount up to the overs limit.

As a simple example, let's say that you and I are in a $2/$4 game and we'd like to play a higher limit, but no such game is available. Let's say that we agree that we would like to bet $16 when there's just the two of us in the game. The dealer gives us a button identifying us as overs players and at the beginning of the first betting round when there's just the two of us in the hand, the limit is $16.

The good thing about this is that this new higher limit will never affect anyone at the table who does not want to be an overs player. As long as there's a non-overs player in the game, the limit will remain at $2/$4. This is a good situation for you because you're the better player getting the worse player to occasionally play at a higher limit. You'll also have the added advantage in that he'll usually forget he's an overs player when he first looks at his two hole cards. He'll usually be playing hands that he thinks are good for $2/$4, but he wouldn't want to be calling $16 with them on the river. The higher limit also reduces the impact of the rake.

At what stage of a hand does the overs limit become the new limit?

I've received a lot of email on this because it can be confusing and it needs to be addressed. Consider this scenario:

It's the turn. Players A and B, who are overs players, are in the hand along with Player C, who is not an overs player. Player A bets $4, Player B raises $4 more and Player C folds. Player A must fold, call the $4 raise or raise $4 more. He cannot call the $4 and then raise $16 more, even though the only two players remaining are overs players.

The overs limit comes into effect only at the beginning of a betting round. The betting limit cannot change in the middle of a betting round. Since there was a non-overs player in the hand at the beginning of the betting on the turn, the limit must remain at $4 for all of the action on the turn.

However, when the river cards comes, and there are only overs players in the hand at the beginning of the betting round, then the round can be bet at the overs limit.

Okay, there are only us two overs players in the hand at the beginning of this betting round. Do I *have* to bet the overs amount or can I just bet the $4?
Playing the overs is not mandatory. It is only an option. If your only opponent is an overs player and he bets first, he can bet either $4 or $16. If he chooses to bet only $4, you can then raise either $4 or $16, but once there's been a $16 bet, you both can only bet or raise $16 from that point on.

I want to remind you that there's no disgrace in stepping down in limit for a while if you have to. It's great to be able to play in a game you know you can beat. If you're having a bad run at $10/$20 or $1/$2 no-limit, it will do you good to play in a game you're sure to beat. This win won't be as big, but it will be a win. And I think the best part about playing low limit for a while is what it does for your confidence.

5.
PROFITING FROM MISTAKES

Poker is a zero-sum game. That means that one player's win is another player's loss, and vice versa. If you win $100 playing heads-up poker, that means your opponents had to have lost that much money to you. The money had to come from somewhere. If 10 players each buy into the game with $100, then that $1,000 will be distributed in different amounts among those 10 players. After many hours of play, there will still be $1,000 on the table, only it might be in the hands of three winners and seven losers. (This example assumes there is no rake or dealer tipping.)

In the short run, the random distribution of the cards will determine who the winners and losers are among equally skilled players. You could be the worst player in the game but if you get hit with the deck the first hour of play, you will be a huge winner and most of the other players will be losers. You'll look like a very successful poker player. But, that's not the way poker works. Play long enough, and everyone will eventually get the same hands in the same positions as every other player. Everyone would then have about the same amount of money in the game.

Yet, we all know that some players are consistent winners and most players are consistent losers. Why is that? It's because poker is a game of skill where you use poker chips to keep score. In the long run, the players who accumulate the most chips always turn out to be the most skillful, knowledgeable and talented players. That's because poker is a game of mistakes and the players who make fewer mistakes than their opponents will eventually get all the money.

Your job, therefore, is to learn all about the mistakes that can be made in poker, and then learn how to correct them or avoid making them altogether. The following chapters will help you with that task. They include a rather lengthy, but not necessarily all-inclusive list of mistakes that beginners make.

It will definitely help you to study these mistakes and to review it regularly as you learn how to play poker. The lists will be helpful in at least two ways: They will help you recognize and fix the mistakes you're making right now, and they will help you see some of the mistakes your opponents make.

Anytime a player makes a mistake that you don't make, you profit. Make that your goal.

6.
MISTAKES MADE
BEFORE THE GAME

1. NOT THINKING ABOUT POKER ON THE WAY TO THE GAME

Not thinking about poker away from the game is the equivalent of not warming up before you run the 100-yard dash, lift weights or swim competitively. It's important that you mentally change gears and have your mind totally on poker when you take that seat. Have you ever seen the intense warm-up routine of boxers right before the first-round bell rings? They do it because it works. And so should you. You should be thinking about the other players, what your strategy is going to be, and anticipating which common situations are going to arise as soon as you start playing. You need to mentally gear up for the game.

Ken, I recognize the importance of the above advice but I really don't want to get that deep into what's just a really fun game for me. Is there just one easy thing I could do to keep from making this mistake?
You could take the time and effort to decide in advance which hands you will and will not play for your first hand, and in which positions, besides being in the blinds. A possible suggestion might be, "I won't play a hand unless both of my hole cards are a 10 or higher." Another suggestion might be, "I'm not going to play the blinds unless I get A♠ A♦, K♠ K♥, Q♦ Q♥, J♣ J♠ or A♥ K♥. Use whatever guideline works for you, but

at least take the time to give it some thought before the game. Even some, simple, basic guidelines are better than none at all.

Researchers in the know have determined that it is very useful and beneficial for you to review your game plan in your mind the night before you intend to play. This gives your subconscious time to digest and absorb the information. This, in turn, makes it easier for you to remember and implement your plan.

2. NOT KNOWING WHAT EVERYONE ELSE KNOWS ABOUT THE GAME

Poker is all about how you collect and use concealed information, having skills that the other players don't have, and generally disguising your poker genius. When you sit down in a game, you're matching wits with nine other players all at the same time. It's as if all nine of them got together to play against you.

That's a tall order, to win under those circumstances. Poker today is very different than poker in the past. Players have access to computers that play poker, an endless number of opponents on Internet poker sites, dozens of magazines devoted exclusively to the game, hundreds of new poker books — many of them written by world champion poker players and others written by some of the most brilliant minds in the world — and an endless showing of poker on television. World-class professional poker players are also dispensing advice practically for free to anyone who'll take the time to absorb it. There is no shortage of ways that a student can learn to play poker. When you take a seat in a game, you're playing against players who have been exposed to all of this. Collectively, they undoubtedly have a greater understanding of the game than you do.

It makes for an uneven playing field, but there's a way you can level that field. You do not have to quit your day job to become a full-time poker student. There's a principle that's taught in the management field that's called "The 80-20 Rule." It means that you can accomplish 80 percent of your goal with only 20 percent of your maximum effort. It applies to almost anything you do in life, and you can apply it to your poker education. Most good poker players have read one or more of the same basic core of poker books. If you have never read a poker book, you can catch up with your opponents just by reading two or three of the better ones—you don't have to read the top fifty poker books. If you've never played poker online, you'd benefit a lot by playing just a few hours—you don't have to play nonstop for a month. And if you've never read a poker magazine, all you need to do is look at a couple of issues and *voilà!*—you're now as smart as your average opponent.

3. MINIMIZING MISTAKES

Poker is a game of mistakes and whoever makes the fewest mistakes will be the winner. As you read the rest of this list of mistakes that beginners make, you'll see they all have their roots in this fundamental idea.

Not making mistakes is the very definition of skill at poker. Of course, the first step is to become aware of what those mistakes are. Most beginners incorrectly think that their profit comes from making big hands and winning big pots. They don't yet realize that the real profit comes from simply making good decisions.

4. ABUSING ALCOHOL AND DRUGS
I'm not going to beat a dead horse over this issue. You already know that you have to have a clear mind when you play poker. After all, it's really your only weapon.

5. NOT KNOWING WHERE YOUR PROFIT COMES FROM IN A POKER GAME
Your profit comes from the mistakes your opponents make. This is why you can't win in the long term when you play against superior talent. The advice here is simple: Play against weaker opponents, ones you *can* beat.

6. NOT KNOWING WHAT YOUR THEORETICAL GOAL SHOULD BE AND THEN KNOWING HOW TO CHOOSE A STRATEGY TO ACCOMPLISH THAT GOAL
It is important to understand the strategy and tactics of poker. Before reading further, do you know the difference between strategy and tactics?

A strategy is the big, overall goal that you're trying to accomplish. A tactic is the exact, specific way or means by which you accomplish that goal. In a war, a strategy might be to destroy an enemy bridge. The tactic you use to accomplish that strategy might be to bomb it from the air or, as a second tactic, to send in a demolition team to dynamite it. There are usually many different tactics available to support a single strategy.

In poker, your strategy might be to get a player to fold. Do you use the tactic of betting into him, check-raising him, or waiting for the turn to bet when the bets double? In another case, your strategy might be to make the pot as big as possible. Do you use the tactic of betting, raising, or check-raising?

There's a point in the education of every poker player where even just the awareness that these poker questions exist are new to him. I assure you that there was a time when Johnny Chan, Doyle Brunson and Chris Moneymaker didn't know a check from a check-raise. They learned and so will you. You have to first learn what you're trying to accomplish, otherwise you won't know for sure what your strategy should be or which tactics you should choose to implement your plan.

7. BEING RESULT-ORIENTED

I believe that the nature of today's society has been changed so much by the proliferation of computers, poker books, poker sites, and the explosion of the information age that they have all conspired to eliminate result-oriented learning as a problem. At least it's not as prevalent as it was even twenty years ago.

What is being result-oriented? It can be summed up by saying "Well, I must have done the right thing because I got the result I wanted," or "I must have done the wrong thing because I didn't get the result I wanted." It's the trial-and-error method of learning. In poker, as in most other areas in life, you can do the wrong thing and still win. And you can do the right thing and still lose. There are poker players who win hands without knowing that they played it the wrong way. And because of that, they think that how they played it was the right thing to do. They will remember that and that's how they'll play that same hand in future situations.

You need to understand that the most important poker skill you can have is to know what the right thing is to do and then go through with it. Your actual results don't matter. Your goal is to consistently do the right thing regardless of the result because you know it's the most profitable thing to do in the long run.

To sum up, it's the *process,* not the result, that you should focus on. Good results are nice and they make you feel good, but you should derive even more satisfaction from knowing you made the best decision regardless of the result. This chapter will help you develop a thought process that will prevent negative results while you're learning the game.

8. NOT KNOWING THE BASIC MATH OF HOLD'EM

Limit hold'em is a game of patience and mathematics. Fortunately, the math is simple once you learn the basics. The number of cards in the deck will never change. You'll always be dealt only two cards. There will always be exactly three cards on the flop, the odds of making a set, a straight, a flush and all the other hands will always be the same, and the size of the bets don't change.

Math scares off a lot of players, so let me restate this in other words so I don't lose you: Every decision you will ever make in a limit hold'em game will be based partly on the mathematics of the situation. The good news is that these situations are so repetitive that and you won't have any problem learning the math simply because the same common situations occur over and over with each hand. If you'll take the time to memorize the 10 most common hold'em math facts, you'll know almost everything you need to know about math. It's that easy.

You do not have to be a wizard at math to hold your own against your average opponents. You can even apply the 80-20 Rule I mentioned in Mistake #2, earlier. If you'll just take the time to give the chapter a cursory look, and just hit the highlights, you'll easily get 80 percent of it with just a little effort.

9. INCORRECT STARTING HAND SELECTION

There's guidance elsewhere in this book on how to choose two good cards to play. Some of the more important mistakes to avoid when deciding which hands to play are:

• Not Recognizing the Importance of Gaps

A gap is a hole between your two cards. If you hold Q♠ 10♥, you have one gap in your hand. K♠ 10♥ has two gaps.

The problem with these hands is that you have to hit exactly one card on the flop to have a possible straight draw with a one-gap hand and you need to get the exact two cards you need in a two-gap hand. This makes straight draws with gaps harder to make than hands with no gaps.

• Not Giving Thought to Your Kicker
If you play an ace, you're going to need a big kicker, especially if the field is huge. Same with a king. K♣ 8♦ is not a good hand even if you flop another king. Anyone else holding a king could have a better kicker than you.

• Playing One Big Card and One Little Card
What are you trying to make when you play hands like K♠ 5♦, Q♥ 4♠ and J♥ 3♣? Look at it this way: If you deliberately choose to play a hand with one useless card, then you're really playing 6-card poker while everyone else in the game is playing 7-card poker.

10. NOT REALIZING THAT A HAND'S VALUE DEPENDS ON THE CIRCUMSTANCES
I like to say that a hand's value is both situational and relative. You cannot play every hand the same way from every position all the time. A♥ 10♥ on the button when everyone has folded preflop is not the same when it's been raised and reraised before the flop and you're in the 5-seat. K♠ 9♣ does not have the same value on the button as it does under the gun (first to act after the big blind). The strength and value of each hand depends on your position, the number of players

before and after you, the action, the probable action after you, and several other factors. This means that you have to evaluate the same hand differently depending on the circumstances. This means that it is wrong to make automatic plays.

11. NOT RECOGNIZING THE IMPORTANCE OF THE CONCEPT OF DOMINATED HANDS OR KNOWING WHEN YOUR HAND IS DOMINATED

To have a dominated hand is to have a hand that is markedly inferior to a like, but similar, hand heads-up. A♦ Q♥ is a dominated hand when your opponent holds A♣ K♦. You are about a 4 to 1 underdog with that hand. Your hand is also dominated when you hold a pocket pair, but your opponent holds a higher pocket pair. You can save a lot of money when you can figure out when you're in these types of situations and you're disciplined enough to let the hand go.

What's the quickest and easiest way that I can apply this lesson and therefore save the most money?
Since most raising hands that your opponents will have will be A♠ K♥ or a high pocket pair, you can stop calling preflop raises with A-9 down through A-2. When you go through the list of his probable raising hands, you'll see that your A♦ 9♣, A♥ 6♠, K♦ Q♣, K♥ J♠, Q♣ J♥, Q♦ 10♠ and even small pocket pairs will be losers in the long run. Let your hand go, let the raiser win this one time, and save your money for those times when you have A♥ K♣ or a big pair and *you* want to be the raiser.

12. NOT ADJUSTING TO THE NUMBER OF PLAYERS IN THE HAND

There are two factors that work hand-in-hand in determining your chances of winning a hand. The first is the actual cards you hold, and the second is the number of players there are in the hand against you. Some hands play better against one or a few players and some hands are more profitable when everyone's in on the hand. J♦ 10♦ is a horrible hand to play against two players, but it's awesomely profitable when you have it on the button with nine-way action.

The number of players in the hand affects your chances of winning by having the best hand, winning by having all the other players miss their draws, or winning by bluffing on the river. The more players there are in the hand, the less often you will win and that in turn contributes to your negative swings in the game.

A very common mistake beginners make is that they don't realize the significance of what the dealer is telling them when he says, "X number of players," when the action is complete before the flop. The greater the number of players in the hand, the better the flop has to be for you. The value of good starting hands goes down in value rapidly as each new player enters the pot to see the flop.

For example, if you have A♦ A♥ heads-up, you're typically a 4 to 1 favorite. However, if it's you against four other players, you are now a 2 to 1 underdog to win the hand, even though you have the best hand and you're a favorite against any one of them individually.

Is there some way that I can immediately apply this lesson, fix this mistake and win more money?
Yes. One of the more common mistakes that beginners make is that they limp in before the flop with hands that they should raise with when they are first to enter the pot. Being first in, raising when there are only the blinds and forcing the drawing hands to fold (if they play correctly), vastly increases the chance that you will win the hand. Better to win a medium-sized pot against three players than to lose a large pot against seven players. Many times when you win by raising as the first one in, someone will say after the hand, "I would have won that hand if you hadn't raised before the flop." Good for you.

13. NOT COUNTING THE POT
As you probably already know, all of the decisions you'll make in a poker game center around your cards, the board cards you see, the bet size, and the pot size. You're always going to be computing some kind of odds while you're playing the hand. Most of those decisions will be to weigh the size of the pot against the chance you have of making your hand or winning the hand with what you have. How can you do the math to arrive at a decision if you don't know how much money is in the pot? Seems like a very easy and obvious question, yet most beginning players do not know the importance and necessity of counting the pot.

Fortunately, counting the pot is not that difficult and it easily becomes second-nature once you get in the habit of doing it. That's because you don't have to actually count the pot down to the last chip or last dollar. What you should be counting instead is the number of bets that go into the pot. Count, "1, 2, 3, 4, etc." as each player throws his bet into the pot to call before the flop. If someone raises, count that as two bets because that's what it is. Continue the count for the bets that go into the pot on the flop.

After the action on the flop is complete, divide your running count by two. That's because the size of the bets double on the turn. Twenty-two small bets, for example, then becomes eleven big bets and then you continue counting from eleven starting with the bets that go in on the turn and river. This will always give you the pot odds that you need to know.

Or, you can get a pretty good, though not perfect, idea by looking at the chips in the middle.

14. MAKING A BET WITHOUT INFORMATION ABOUT THE OTHER PLAYERS OR KNOWING WHO'S IN THE HAND

As wild as it sounds, many beginning players do not even look around the table to see who's calling before they act on their hands. You miss everything when you do this. You miss possible tells, you don't have any idea how a player might feel about his hand judging by how he acts (even though he called) — and you miss it when a player almost decides to raise, but only calls. And how do you know what the chances are of you winning the hand if you don't know how many players you're up against? There are some players who play only A♥ K♣, A♦ Q♠, or high cards. Why would you blindly call with any hand if this player called in front of you?

15. NOT RESPECTING POSITION

Playing out of position. The simple and obvious fact that the betting in a poker game takes place in a clockwise motion means that players will always act before the players on their left. The sooner you have to act in a betting round, the better your hand has to be in order to correctly withstand the adverse impact of having to call a raise and therefore play the hand for two bets. Players acting after you have a tremendous advantage over you because they will always know what you've done before they act on their hands, and you'll always have to act on your hand without knowing what they're going to do. This means you won't get to show down a hand for free on the river because you will often have to call a bet after you've checked, and you won't know if it's a value bet or a bluff.

These situations where you have to call a raise here and there, where you can't check and win, and you can't bluff, all have a cumulative effect that adds up over the course of the game. You're going to lose a lot of bets, albeit only one or two at a time, and you're going to have to forfeit a lot of pots because of your bad position. Your loss is the other player's gain.

16. TOO SMALL A BANKROLL FOR THE LIMIT AND TYPE GAME YOU'RE PLAYING

It's not the actual amount of money you buy in for that's too small or not enough. You have to take into consideration how much money it costs to play a hand all the way through to the river. Then you have to assume that you might lose as many as eight or ten hands before you finally win a pot. It's discouraging, but it happens to all of us.

Let's use a $3/$6 game as an example. If it costs $3 to call before the flop, $3 on the flop and $6 each on the turn and river, then you've invested $18 in the hand. Some hands are raised, so you might average investing $24 on each hand you play. As you see, a $100 buy-in gives you only enough ammunition to play four, or maybe five, hands. That's not enough.

You should buy in for about fifty times the size of the big blind. So if you're playing $3/$6, you should buy in for about $300; and if you're playing $10/$20, make your buy-in for about $1,000. That will give you enough chips to withstand some losses and still have enough chips to play good poker.

If you're a good player and you lose a $100 buy-in in just a few hands, it might just be because you're actually in a very good game! If you're in a game with some very loose, wild and crazy players, then this is an extremely profitable situation for you. You might have just suffered a few bad beats by some very unlikely longshot draws getting there, played by some bad players. You will be a winner in the long run against these types of players if you can stay in the game long enough to win a few hands, win a big pot or two, and let the element of skill slowly overtake the short-term element of luck. In games like this, be prepared for some big swings and be willing to stay in the game for a long time. On the other hand, if it's you who are the bad player, no buy-in will ever be big enough to guarantee that you'll be a winner.

One thing you can do to help avoid being identified as a beginner is to take all of your chips out of the rack. You'll blend in more easily this way.

17. GOING ALL IN IN AN INCORRECT MANNER

There's a common all-in situation that most players eventually face sooner or later and almost all of them handle it incorrectly. That's when you have fewer chips left than what it would normally take to play a good hand all the way to the river. For example, you have $14 in chips in front of you in a $3/$6 hold'em game. Most players just call their chips away, go all-in before the hand is over and hope to win. This is wrong!

What they should be doing is raising before the flop to make players who might otherwise call one bet fold when they are faced with having to call two bets. This is to reduce the number of players who call to see the flop. If you just call before the flop, you might be facing six opponents, which gives you a 14 percent chance of winning the pot. If you raise preflop, you might be facing only two opponents, which gives you a 33 percent chance of winning the pot. And here's the main point: Since all of your remaining money is going in on this hand anyway, why not give yourself the best chance to win the hand. If you win the hand and then someone says, "I would have won that hand except for the fact that I didn't want to call two bets cold," then you know you did the right thing.

18. PLAYING TOO MANY HANDS

Strangely, almost no one ever plays too few hands. Why does everyone always seem to play too many hands? It's because it is true that any two cards can win and we've all seen it. Everyone also knows that the good hands are A♦ A♣, K♥ K♠, Q♠ Q♦, A♦ K♥ and so on. They also know that the bad hands are 7♣ 2♠, 10♥ 3♠, Q♦ 4♥ and the like. The problem arises when it comes to judging all those other hands in the middle.

The answer lies in the simple fact that a lot of hands that look pretty are not winners in the long run. This almost always makes those middle range hands even bigger losers than they were in the beginning. When you constantly play weak hands just to be in action, you're going to be a permanent loser. It's tough to do, and it's very boring, but you have to play only the highest hands in the long run to be a winner at this game. It means you'll have to fold and sit out as many as 85 percent of the hands you're dealt. Beginners are losers because that's just one of the many things they can't yet do. That also means that you shouldn't play every suited ace just because it's suited.

19. PLAYING TOO AGGRESSIVELY

Betting when you should check, and raising when you should be only calling, are costly moves. Playing too aggressively means trying to take control of the hand when your cards or your position don't warrant it. It's overplaying your hand for value when you don't actually have the value. It is not the same thing as bluffing. What happens when you're identified as being too aggressive is that your opponents will start checking their better hands to you in order to let you continue putting money in the pot when you have a loser—but don't know it. Overaggressiveness also sets you up for being slowplayed and check-raised.

20. PLAYING TOO PASSIVELY

This is the opposite of playing too aggressively. It means folding when you should call, checking when you should bet, and calling when you should be raising. Not betting when you should is one of the worst mistakes a player can make in any form of poker. It allows other players to draw out on you for free, it sets you up to be bluffed out of the hand, and you don't get full value for your hand when you do win.

Recently, I played in a hold'em game with a woman who seemed to be an otherwise good player, except for the fact that she was afraid to bet her good hands. She wanted to win the hand, but at the cheapest price. For example, she limped in from fourth position and saw a flop in an unraised pot with eight total players. The flop was Q♠ 7♦ 4♣. It was bet and she called, as did six other players. The turn was the 2♦. She checked and called. The river was the A♥.

BOARD

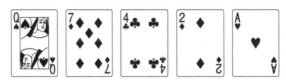

She checked and called again. She was holding Q♦ Q♥! At no time did she bet for value, raise to protect her hand, or bet on the end to extract bets from worse hands.

A few hands later, the board was 10♠ 7♦ 5♣ 5♥ 2♥, and she played the same way. She checked and called down to the river. What do you think she had? Since I had already figured out how she played, I was the only one at the table not surprised when she turned over 7♣ 7♠ and won the pot with a full house.

Do you see the problem with playing like this? You don't get full value from your hands when you play passively. You can't be a winner if you can't use your winning hands to make up for the money you lose on your losing hands. However, it's great for you if there's a passive player like this in your game. She could have extracted extra bets before and after the flop with both of those hands and those extra bets stayed in my stack instead of moving over to her stack.

21. GOING ON TILT

Going *on tilt* is simply the term for what's happening when you let you emotions control your decision-making process. That is, losing your discipline. This costs poker players more money than any other one weakness there is. There's something in all of us that disrupts the reasoning process and motivation to play perfectly when something bad happens in the game. It's difficult enough to play perfectly all the time so it takes very little to make a player voluntarily surrender his will to play the right way. It's as if we're all looking for any excuse to start playing every hand, calling every bet, and not caring how the hand turns out. This is a very difficult weakness to correct because it takes the utmost in self-awareness, discipline and desire to fix it.

There are probably as many different solutions to the problem as there are players. Going on tilt is a deeply psychological reaction to a stimuli. Every poker player has to handle it in his own way. I suppose the best advice that I could give for a temporary, quick fix is to quote Mike Caro, "It's okay to always play your best game."

If there could ever be such a thing as a one-sided coin in poker, then going on tilt would be it. Going on tilt always makes you play worse and never makes you play better. If you'd had a bad beat or two that makes you want to play recklessly, try to get a handle on it. The first step is to realize what's happening to you. If you must react by playing differently (worse), try to find ways that aren't totally stupid. Try to be selective. Raise with calling hands, be more aggressive and bluff more, but don't do it with totally worthless hole cards.

22. DELIBERATELY PLAYING HANDS THAT YOU KNOW ARE UNPROFITABLE IN THE LONG RUN

A beginner will usually make a mistake without knowing it's a mistake. However, many beginners will deviate from what they know is the best way to play anyway. They think of all the ways that they could vary their play, then deliberately play losing hands. As one player told me when he made a full house with an 8♣ 5♥, "I like to zig and zag so nobody can put me on a hand." What he doesn't realize is that if he plays hands with a negative expectation, it doesn't matter if anyone puts him on a hand or not—for that one, specific hand. The longer you play a certain way—winning or losing—the more certain it is that you will eventually experience the true results of that play. In other words, the longer you've been playing poker, the more certain it is that your overall win/loss record is an accurate indication of your true poker skill.

The average beginner who knowingly plays a bad hand does so in the very incorrect belief that he can win a much bigger pot than usual if he gets lucky and hits his hand. This is partially true to a certain extent—for that one hand only. The problem is that the pot will never be big enough to make up for the other bad hands he played and did not win.

23. DELIBERATELY PLAYING BADLY

This is not necessarily the same thing as playing bad hands, as mentioned above. This is a much worse mistake. A player who plays bad hands on purpose could also be an otherwise good player with just that one bad habit. But, if you deliberately play poker badly, then you are doing everything wrong. Choosing the wrong strategy and tactics, ignoring the odds, and deliberately throwing money away is far more costly than just playing two inferior cards. If this is how you play, then you're not going to last very long as a poker player.

24. NOT BEING WILLING TO LEARN SHORT-HANDED PLAY

Being able to play short-handed poker correctly is one of the toughest things that a player can learn how to do. It requires a lot of practice, study and experience. I don't blame beginners for not wanting to play short-handed. The blinds come around quickly, you rarely get a good hand, the rake takes a lot of your money, and you never have the odds to draw to straights and flushes. Short-handed play places a premium on hand-reading skills and a willingness to play much looser while bluffing a lot and calling with very weak hands. Who wants to play like that? Not your average beginner, that's for sure.

However, there are a couple of times when you should consider playing short-handed. The first is when you'd like to get in a little short-handed practice. After all, you can leave the game at any time if you decide you're in over your head. The other time is when the game is four-handed and you're playing at that time of day when you know other poker players will soon be coming in to play. You can then add one player at a time to the game as they come in and the game will quickly fill up.

25. NOT CAPPING THE BETTING WITH PREMIUM HANDS

It's okay to limp in before the flop with the best hands in hold'em—A♠ A♣, K♥ K♦, Q♦ Q♠ or A-Ks—if that's the way you want to play it. You disguise your strength, you can check-raise on the flop with the best hand or you can muck the hand on the flop if you have to, knowing that you've invested only one small bet on the hand. Hey, pocket aces don't survive every flop and win every hand anyway! No problem. However, the problem arises when the betting is raised before the flop and you have A♠ A♦, K♦ K♥, Q♣ Q♠ or A-Ks and you don't go ahead and raise and reraise up to the maximum number of bets.

This is where it pays to focus on the long-term. There are no other hands in hold'em that will win more money than A♠ A♥ and K♦ K♠. Once the raising starts, you make far more money in the long run by raising with these hands than you do by trying to disguise your hand for only one more bet. You want more chips in the pot in a hand in which you will be the winner most of the time.

7.
MISTAKES MADE BEFORE THE FLOP

26. NOT HAVING BASIC HAND-READING SKILLS

I don't blame beginners for not being skilled at reading other player's hands. That's a skill that takes thousands of hands over the course of several years to fine tune. Where beginners are falling down on the job is that they don't actually begin the process of learning beginning hand-reading skills or give any thought at all what their opponents might be holding. All they do is look at their cards, look at the board, and then decide whether to bet, check or fold.

Once you learn the basics of how the game is dealt, you should then start to become aware of what's going on around you. You should be aware of who's in the hand with you and what kind of cards your opponents *might* be holding. You don't even have to know for sure—all you have to do is start to give it some kind of thought during the play of the hand. Like all the other skills you need to be a good player, you'll learn hand reading in due course with practice and experience.

27. NOT PLAYING DIFFERENT PLAYERS DIFFERENTLY

Everybody has their own idea of what constitutes a good poker hand. That's what makes poker a great game. Some players will *always* play a certain hand the same way while other players would *never* play that hand at all. Some players will always raise with certain hands and not others, and some other players will never bluff or always bluff. All you have to do is remember who likes to do what and who can be relied on to always, or at least generally, play the same way. That's not as large a task as it might initially sound. You'll usually be playing against the same people most of the time and you'll easily learn their habits through sheer repetition. It'll start to come to you as second nature whenever you're in a hand with certain players. All you have to do to improve as a poker player is just realize this simple fact and give some thought to what you know about how *that* player would play that hand.

Way back in the early 1980s, when I was a rank beginner at poker, I sat down in a game in a public cardroom in the Seattle area. Being a beginner who just liked to play, and one who made most of the mistakes you're reading about in this chapter, I never even looked at the player's faces. After about thirty minutes, there was a pause in the action (I must have been dealt 7♦ 2♥ and missed the flop), and I took a minute to look up and look around the table at my fellow players. And suddenly, before I could stop myself, I blurted out, "Hey, aren't you Tim Conway?" (it was) and as quick as a shot he replied, "I'd better be—I'm wearing his underwear!"

> Note: As this chapter progresses, the explanations to the mistakes that beginners make will be shorter. That's because—as you may have realized by now—many mistakes are interrelated. Many big mistakes consist of several smaller supporting mistakes. If you understand what's been said up to this point, and then add to that understanding as you read on, each mistake and explanation will be obvious. I hope.

28. NOT FOLDING WHEN IT'S CLEAR YOUR HAND IS DOMINATED

You won't always know for sure, unless you're calling a raise from a player who only raises with A♥ A♦, K♦ K♣, Q♠ Q♥ or A♦ K♦. Or did you not realize that there are players who will raise only with these hands? If you pay attention to who raises and what they've raised with in the past, you can learn to profitably fold hands like A♦ J♥, A♠ 10♣, K♣ Q♠ and K♠ J♥ before the flop—if you can accurately determine that it's the right, specific time to do so. There are other players whose raising requirements are so loose that you could even reraise with these hands. You just have to know your players.

29. NOT KNOWING WHEN A♦ K♥ IS THE BEST HAND

It doesn't take a full house to win every hand. Because of the community card nature of the game, you're really only betting on the difference between your two hole cards and your opponent's two hold cards. There will be times the flop will miss both of you and A♦ K♥ will be the best hand. When you see the flop nine-handed with A♦ K♥, it's a drawing hand. You're just going to have to improve the hand to win. But when you're heads-up and you've raised before the flop, there's a good chance that you're going to still have the best hand after the flop. And even if your opponent has you only slightly beat, you still might win by betting on the flop and forcing him to fold. Learn to not automatically fold or think you don't have a hand if you miss the flop with A♠ K♦ — you often will have the best hand at this point or make a hand by the river.

When you raise before the flop with A♦ K♥, and a caller calls your raise cold without reraising, he will usually have two high cards that are not a pair. He'll have hands like A♠ Q♦, A♦ J♣, A♣ 10♥, K♥ Q♠, K♠ J♦, K♦ 10♣, Q♣ J♥, Q♥ 10♠ and J♠ 10♦. Have I named a hand yet that beats A♦ K♥? No. So, when the flop does not contain a queen, jack or 10, you still have the best hand. It's just a matter of comparing your hole cards to his probable hand. If the flop has an ace or a king, you make a big pair and you still have the best hand. You don't have to fear the flop or worry about scare cards. Make sure you bet on the flop to give him a chance to either muck his hand or make a mistake by calling with the worst hand.

When you raise preflop with A♦ K♠ and you get called by a sole opponent who you know would only call with high cards, you still have the best hand if the flop is:

9♠ 7♦ 4♣, 8♥ 6♠ 2♦, 7♣ 7♥ 5♠ or 5♦ 4♣ 3♥. Don't be afraid to bet.

30. CALLING PREFLOP RAISES RATHER THAN RAISING OR FOLDING

Beginners usually have to be taught that raising is often a superior move to either folding or calling. Assume you have a hand that has a 20 percent chance of winning in a four-handed pot. If you fold, you lose what you've invested in the hand. If you call, you will lose four out of five times, along with a lot of your chips. However, if you raise, you might get it heads-up and then have a 45 percent chance of winning. Your raise might also buy you a free card—or two—and you might just win the pot right there. The advice here is to just simply ask yourself if raising might be a better option the next time you're thinking of calling or folding.

31. COLD CALLING PREFLOP RAISES

Cold calling is one of the most frequent, costly, and common blunders that the average beginner makes in hold'em. Since most beginners already make the mistake of playing hands that aren't even worth one bet, they will often go ahead and play the hand for two or more bets before the flop. When you have no money in the pot and it's on you to call two or more bets cold, you have very little incentive or reason to play this hand. I'm talking, of course, about average hands, and not reraising monsters like A♠ A♣ or K♦ K♥. The preflop raise should tell you something. I've found a very good way

97

to explain this concept to my students that they seem to like, so here it is:

Nobody wins every single hand. The starting hands are distributed at random. It is mainly just the value of the cards themselves that determine whether or not there will be a preflop raise. The player in the seat that raised got a little bit lucky for this hand only. His raise tells you that he has a much better than average hand. He, therefore, has a better than average chance of winning this hand. You will probably lose money to this player in the long run under these circumstances. So, why don't you sit this hand out, let him be the winner (since it seems to be somewhat predetermined that he will be the winner), and save your money for the times when you have the preflop raising hand.

Look at it this way: Would you rather put two bets in the pot when another player wants you to (and you don't know what he has), or would you rather put those two bets in the pot when *you* want to raise because you know what you have and he doesn't?

That just seems to be a better time to put your money in action, given the small amount of information you have at this point. Learn to take turns winning. Even Muhammad Ali knew when to duck. Take the big, long term view of the game and while you should try to win every hand that you can, be sensible about folding when it looks like you can't.

This is what Phil Hellmuth is bragging about when he says, "I can dodge bullets, baby!" He's right.

Of all the advice I give beginners, this is the one that they are most impressed with because it works for them.

32. ALWAYS CALLING A RAISE IN THE SAME BETTING ROUND AFTER LIMPING IN

The mistake made here is in the word *always*. This is when you limp in for the small bet and then it's raised behind you. You do not have to always automatically call that raise. There are several factors at work here: The raiser probably has you beat and dominated already, there may be another raise before the round is over, other players may fold—thereby reducing your pot and implied odds—and it is almost always going to cost you a lot more money to play the hand to the end. Try to fold those hands that you know are sure losers and cut your losses right there.

This is one of those few times where even the professionals differ wildly on how to handle this situation. Most lean toward calling anyway if their call will close out the betting. That means that the raiser is the first player on his immediate left. Other pros will call or fold according to how many other players also call the raise and some pros will almost always call anyway because they're looking for help from the flop.

The main idea that you need to take away from this is that you should not get in the habit of making automatic plays. You always have time to stop and think about what's best for you. It's just that if you're a typical beginner, you are most certainly calling too much in this situation. Stop that!

33. NOT RAISING WHEN YOU'RE THE FIRST TO ENTER THE POT

High cards and high pairs play best in early position where you can raise and make it incorrect for the players behind you to see the flop. Lower ranking cards need many players in the pot in order to have the correct odds to draw to their hands and to make up for the fact that they are dominated 4 to 1. When you just call in early position, you are inviting each and every opponent to beat you for the smallest possible price. Better to have a high chance of winning a small pot than very little chance of winning a big pot. And if you get lucky, you'll have a big chance of winning a big pot.

Exercise

For an entire playing session, you should always come in raising if you're first to enter the pot. This will give you a lot of experience with this tactic in a very short period of time. You'll be able to drive the point home quickly and you'll see the benefits immediately. But beware. After it becomes evident to the other players that this is going to be your usual manner of play, they will start to adjust to you. They will start folding worse hands preflop and check-raising you with their better hands. And possibly—eventually—they just might ignore you altogether and not make any adjustments at all. This is a good exercise because you'll quickly learn more about poker strategy.

34. RAISING PREFLOP WITH THE WRONG HANDS OR FOR THE WRONG REASONS

A lot of beginners like to raise before the flop just for the sake of building big pots. It's exciting and it makes for a fun game. You should have a specific reason and goal in mind when you make a preflop raise. Any time you play a hand for two or more bets, you really should know what you're doing and why. Otherwise, you're just throwing your money away.

35. CALLING TOO LOOSELY IN THE SMALL BLIND

"It's only one more chip, how can that be wrong?" It's wrong for several reasons, unless you have an obviously strong hand. Some hands are so bad, they're not worth 10 cents, let alone another dollar or two. The fact that you already have part of a bet in the hand is meaningless. A cheap call cannot turn bad cards into good cards and cannot turn a loser into a winner. You need to learn to fold based on the value of the hand you hold, and to avoid calling because it costs only a partial bet. The truth is, it will almost always cost you more bets after you see the flop and you'll be playing a hand that's a loser in the long run. Computer simulations (even though they're not accurate for every situation) have clearly shown that more money is lost by the small blinds than any other position at the table. The second-biggest loser is the big blind. This should prove to you that some hands are losers no matter how much or little it costs to see the flop.

36. NOT REALIZING THE VALUE OF SUITED CARDS IN THE SMALL BLIND

If you do call in the small blind, it should be because you have quality cards, and not because it's cheap. When you're in the small blind, you're at a huge disadvantage because you have a random hand and not necessarily a chosen hand with money committed to the pot, and you're in the worst (first) position. However, you should realize that most of the profit earned by the small blind comes from those times when your cards are suited. It seems that the small blind has to make a flush to compensate for those disadvantages and make a profit. So, the lesson is, if you're going to play in the small blind, play only good hands, and if you have to play any other hands, try to restrict them to suited cards only.

Another bit of good advice is this: If you wouldn't play it for a full bet in some other position, then you shouldn't play it for a partial bet in the blind, either.

37. OVERDEFENDING YOUR BIG BLIND

This is an extension of the above three mistakes. You should know by now all the reasons for not automatically calling raises from the big blind. The fact that you already have a full bet in the pot is a trap—don't fall for it.

38. CALLING A RAISE HEADS-UP WHEN IN THE BIG BLIND

This is not the same thing as overdefending the blind. Sometimes everyone will fold, there will be a raise, and the rest of the players will all fold around to you. It's just you in the big blind and the raiser sitting across from you. Most beginners actually handle this situation pretty well. They'll fold bad hands and call and reraise with good hands, but where they drop the ball is when they have those medium-strength hands in between.

My advice in this spot might surprise you, but here it is: Fold all but your obvious reraising hands.

There are a lot of good reasons why you, as a beginner, don't want to get involved in this spot, even with a good-looking hand. Here they are:

1. You're out of position because you'll be first to act on every round with an inferior hand.

2. You don't know for sure where you stand in the hand.

3. You're probably too inexperienced to expertly read his hand and therefore don't know for certain what the correct play will be.

4. The hand will be costly to play.

5. You're getting only 1 to 1 pot odds for bets after the flop.

6. You're probably fighting a maximum rake because of the eventual pot size.

All of these reasons taken together are just too much for a beginner to overcome. You only have one bet in the pot—let it go. Let the raiser win this hand and you can win the next one.

I realize there will be times when you'll have a very good hand in this spot and you might have a very reasonable call. But I still recommend you fold these hands most of the time until you get much better at reading hands and reading your opponents. You'll be in this position so seldom that you're not sacrificing too much. I think it's more important that you save these bets for the hands where you do know exactly what you're doing—while you're still learning the game.

You might be in this particular situation only once per playing session, but it can cost you as much as one-third of your original buy-in if you misplay the hand. My advice is to entirely avoid the situation unless you somehow know for sure exactly where you stand.

39. INCORRECT RAISING FROM THE BLINDS

How many times have you been in the big blind and looked down and saw J♣ J♠, 10♦ 10♥, 9♦ 9♠, or Q♣ J♣ and decided to raise from the big blind position? Probably too many times if you're a beginner. That's because you don't realize what a huge disadvantage it is to be in the blinds. You're first to act on every betting round and now you're playing the hand for two bets. And who knows if you're going to be reraised or not?

Why voluntarily handicap yourself without a great hand to make up for it. The only hands that you can safely and profitably raise with from the blinds are pocket aces and kings; I'm not even sure about pocket queens. I usually go ahead and check in the blinds with pocket queens to see if I get an overcard or flop a set. Sometimes an ace and a king will come on the flop and I can get away from the hand for only one small bet. Raising before the flop with any hand ties you to the pot and makes it harder to fold when it's the correct thing to do.

40. PLAYING ALL SUITED ACES

This is all about being dominated by a player holding an ace with a higher kicker and not having enough players in the hand in order to have the correct odds to draw to a flush. It is a fact that not all suited aces are profitable all the time in all circumstances. It's okay to fold A♠ 4♠ against a preflop raise or when it's heads-up or three-handed. You're not going to make a flush more than 90 percent of the time. So, that means that playing A♠ 4♠ heads-up against a raise is the same thing as playing A♠ 4♣ 90 percent of the time. The bets you save will add up and you'll have that money available when you need to raise with A♠ K♠. It should be obvious that the problem with playing all suited aces is the fact that you have kicker problems when you hold ace-little suited and miss your flush.

41. PLAYING ALL SUITED HANDS

When the President Casino opened their poker room in the summer of 1992, there was a hold'em player who came in from Mobile, Alabama to play on weekends. He announced that he was a pro and he bought in for $500 when every other player's buy-in was only $100 for this $3/$6 game. In the first hour of the game, he raised before the flop at least twenty of the thirty hands he was dealt.

Someone finally asked him, "You can't be getting pocket aces every hand, can you?"

He cheerfully replied, "Oh, no. It's you guys who are not raising enough. Don't you know that you're supposed to raise every time you get an ace, every time you get a pocket pair, every time you're suited and every time you get two connected cards?"

He was serious but it was good for a laugh. You should be able to see the flaw in that raising strategy by now. And he was always the first one to go broke in the game. Oh well, someone has to pay the rake.

42. NOT RAISING ENOUGH FROM THE BUTTON

Remember the earlier advice about how raising might be a better move than just calling or folding? There's another factor that comes into play when you're on the button. You should learn to occasionally raise while on the button with what would otherwise be a calling hand. That's because your extra bet might be returned to you in the form of a free card later in the hand.

There's a tendency for players to respect a raiser and possibly check to him. If you hit the flop, then great! You've gotten in an extra bet with a winning hand. If you miss the flop, it might be checked to you and then you can surprise everyone by checking right behind them. Sometimes you'll get even luckier and they'll check to you again on the turn. You can use the doubled bet on the turn to either drive players out, bet for value, or you can check again. Now you get to see the entire hand for free.

Raising from the button to get a free card is a winning concept for the above reasons.

43. NOT KNOWING THE EQUITY BREAKPOINT FOR YOUR HAND

This is a somewhat advanced concept, but there's no reason a beginner can't be introduced to it. Every hand has an expected value from the pot. For simplicity, let me use an extreme example. You have A♥ A♦ in a $100 pot against a sole opponent who has 7♣ 2♦. Mathematically speaking, your hand is "entitled" to $94 of those $100 and the 7♣ 2♦ gets only $6. It's another way of saying the aces will win 94 percent of the time and the 7♣ 2♦ will win the 6 percent of the time. I think everyone can see the logic in that.

But, suppose you have 10♣ 9♣. What percent of the time do you think you would win when heads-up, or three-handed? How about four-, five-, six-, seven-, eight-, nine- and ten-handed? This is the question you have to answer for every playable hand that you'll ever have, including some unreasonable-looking hands in the blinds. What you're looking for is hands that figure to win more than their fair share of the time for the number of players there are to see the flop with you in the long run. That is, a hand that wins more than 50 percent of the time heads-up or more than 10 percent of the time when it's ten-handed.

Here's a chart that shows the equity breakpoint for each number of players in the hand. It's pretty easy to understand and memorize because it is 100 percent divided by the number of players in the game. The math should look very familiar to you. If not, then keep looking at it until it comes to you.

EQUITY BREAKPOINT BY NUMBER OF PLAYERS

NUMBER OF PLAYERS	EQUITY BREAKPOINT
2	50.0%
3	33.3%
4	25.0%
5	20.0%
6	16.7%
7	14.3%
8	12.5%
9	11.1%
10	10.0%
11	9.1%

You need to learn which hands have a long-term expectation that is greater than their equity breakpoint. These are hands that win more than 50 percent of the time two-handed, 33.3 percent of the time three-handed, 25 percent of the time four-handed, and so on down the chart.

Here's a chart telling you what the equity breakpoint is for pocket pairs. This is a chart of mathematical facts only and does not take into consideration the actual play of the game. This assumes that you play the hand all the way to the river regardless of the action and the board—something you'd never do in a live game. For example, you hold 2♣ 2♦ and the flop is A♥ K♦ Q♠. This chart assumes that you will call to see both the turn and the river in order to catch another deuce, or to possibly win without improving your pocket pair.

ACTUAL EQUITY FOR POCKET PAIRS
(in percentages)

Hands	A-A	K-K	Q-Q	J-J	10-10	9-9	8-8	7-7	6-6	5-5	4-4	3-3	2-2
2	88	85	82	79	77	74	71	68	65	63	60	57	55
3	76	72	68	64	60	56	52	48	45	43	40	37	34
4	68	63	58	54	50	46	43	39	36	33	30	26	22
7	44	39	34	30	27	25	23	21	20	19	17	16	15
10	34	30	26	22	20	18	16	14	13	12	11	10	10

The idea is to compare your hand's actual equity to the equity breakpoint. Whenever you have more equity than you're theoretically entitled to—raise! Since you can see that you'll win the hand more often than your "fair share," you obviously want that pot to be as big as possible. And remember, you're not guaranteed to win any one hand, but you will show a bigger profit in the long run.

Here's the same chart for all the other hands, for ten, seven and four players. You should be able to figure the approximate percentages for five, six, eight and nine players by yourself.

ACTUAL EQUITY FOR FOUR PLAYERS
(in percentages)

	K	Q	J	10	9	8	7	6	5	4	3	2
A	41	39	38	37	36	34	33	31	30	29	28	27
K	–	36	35	33	31	30	28	27	26	25	24	23
Q	–	–	34	32	30	28	26	25	24	23	22	20
J	–	–	–	30	28	26	25	23	23	21	20	19
10	–	–	–	–	27	25	24	22	21	20	19	18
9	–	–	–	–	–	23	22	21	20	19	18	17
8	–	–	–	–	–	–	22	21	19	18	17	16
7	–	–	–	–	–	–	–	21	19	18	17	16
6	–	–	–	–	–	–	–	–	19	18	17	16
5	–	–	–	–	–	–	–	–	–	18	16	15
4	–	–	–	–	–	–	–	–	–	–	16	15
3	–	–	–	–	–	–	–	–	–	–	–	14

ACTUAL EQUITY FOR SEVEN PLAYERS
(in percentages)

	K	Q	J	10	9	8	7	6	5	4	3	2
A	27	25	24	23	21	20	18	17	16	15	14	13
K	–	22	21	19	18	17	16	15	14	13	12	11
Q	–	–	20	18	16	15	14	13	12	10	9	9
J	–	–	–	17	15	14	13	11	10	9	9	8
10	–	–	–	–	14	13	12	11	10	9	8	8
9	–	–	–	–	–	12	11	10	9	8	8	7
8	–	–	–	–	–	–	11	10	9	8	8	7
7	–	–	–	–	–	–	–	10	9	8	8	7
6	–	–	–	–	–	–	–	–	9	8	8	7
5	–	–	–	–	–	–	–	–	–	8	7	6
4	–	–	–	–	–	–	–	–	–	–	7	6
3	–	–	–	–	–	–	–	–	–	–	–	6

ACTUAL EQUITY FOR 10 PLAYERS
(in percentages)

	K	Q	J	10	9	8	7	6	5	4	3	2
A	21	19	17	16	15	14	13	12	11	10	9	8
K	–	17	15	14	13	12	11	10	9	8	8	7
Q	–	–	14	13	11	10	9	9	8	8	7	7
J	–	–	–	11	10	10	9	8	8	7	7	6
10	–	–	–	–	10	9	8	8	7	7	6	6
9	–	–	–	–	–	9	8	7	7	6	6	5
8	–	–	–	–	–	–	8	7	7	6	5	5
7	–	–	–	–	–	–	–	7	6	5	5	4
6	–	–	–	–	–	–	–	–	6	5	4	4
5	–	–	–	–	–	–	–	–	–	5	4	3
4	–	–	–	–	–	–	–	–	–	–	4	3
3	–	–	–	–	–	–	–	–	–	–	–	3

Since you'll make a flush about one in thirty-three times when you're suited, you should add about 3 percent to the above numbers when your two hole cards are suited.

Here are four examples to help you learn how to use the information in the tables in this and the previous section:

1. Look at the equity table for pocket pairs

Look at 2-2 played four-handed. You know that in a four-handed game, the average equity is 25 percent (100/4 = 25). Yet, the equity for 2-2 is 22 percent, a little less than the 25 percent it needs to break even. This tells you that pocket deuces are a slight loser in a four-handed game. This means that you would not want to raise before the flop in the absence of any other information.

2. Look at the equity table for four players

Look at J-9 and let's add 3 percent because we're going to play J♥ 9♥. That gives us an equity of 31 percent, substantially higher than the average fair share of 25 percent. This means that you're going to win with the hand more than if you had random cards, and because of that, you might want to raise before the flop with this hand.

3. Look at the equity table for seven players

I know a player who plays *every* 7♥ 6♣ *every* time in *every* situation. He never throws this hand away before the flop. How do you think this hand is performing for him? You can see that it has an equity of only 10 percent, substantially below the 14.3 percent you'd need to break even in a seven-handed game. By the way, 10 percent is a whopping 30 percent less than 14.3 percent, not 4.3 percent as some of you might think. (10 is only 70 percent of 14.3) This hand is a big loser in the long run in a seven-handed game.

4. Look at the equity table for 10 players

Big slick (A♦ K♠) has an equity of 21 percent where the average share is only 10 percent. If you look again at the equity for pocket pairs you can see that A-K is approximately equal to pocket tens. You have more than twice your fair share of equity; don't be afraid to raise with it before the flop, because you're losing money if you don't.

These percentages are not etched in stone. If you apply a little poker sense, you can see that your actual equity can be more or less depending on your position and other factors in the game.

Exercise

If you understand the concepts presented in Mistake Numbers 40 and 41, then the charts showing your actual hand equity will really be useful to you. You should take the time to go through the charts with a pen or pencil and mark the cutoff hands between positive and negative expectation hands. This will make the charts easier to read and learn the right hands to play.

44. NOT UNDERSTANDING THE EFFECT OF THE RAKE

Most low-limit games are played with a "10 percent/ $5 max" rake. This means that the casino takes $1 for every $10 that goes into the pot up to $5 in a $50 pot. If three players each put $17 in the pot while playing a hand, there will be $51 in the pot. Your potential profit at this point is $34. The house will rake $5, they'll take a $1 jackpot drop, and you'll probably tip the dealer another dollar. Now the pot has only $44 in it, for a net potential profit of only $27 instead of $34. This is *huge*. Did you realize that cuts your profit by a whopping 20 percent? And it happens again over and over as you play all day.

It's like having an unseen eleventh player in the game who wins $5 every hand. At thirty-five hands per hour, that's a rake of $175, or $1,400 in an eight-hour session. Who wins $1,400 a day—every day—at every table in a low-limit game? The house does, that's who. That's a half a million dollars a year—*per table*. This money has to come from somewhere and it comes from you.

This is a big, overlooked concept. When money goes into the pot and is then taken out, it means that you're not being paid your full pot odds. You're being shorted—by the rake. This in turn means you should adjust your pot odds computations by as much as one full bet. It's a small difference, but it is big enough that it adds up over the course of a year of playing.

45. NOT LOOKING FOR THE BEST GAMES

At the lower limits, most of the games available to you are nearly identical. It usually doesn't matter much exactly where you play. The biggest differences will always be the special, unique promotions offered in the poker room and the size and difficulty of hitting the jackpot. You should always be comparison shopping for the best deal. You are spending your hard-earned money on the rake and you should be willing to go wherever the best decision leads you. Take a chance and visit a poker room you've never played in before. Who knows? It just might be your new favorite place to play.

When you're looking at a hold'em game in progress and you're trying to decide whether or not to take a seat, ask yourself one more question: "If I get in this game, which is more likely to happen first if I stay long enough: I'll double my buy-in or I'll lose my buy-in?"

8.
MISTAKES MADE ON THE FLOP

46. NOT ANALYZING THE FLOP

You have A♥ J♠ and the flop is J♦ 9♠ 7♦ with six other players.

YOU

FLOP

Most beginners will say to themselves, "Oh boy, I've got top pair with top kicker!" and blindly wade through the hand. You need to take it at least one step further than that. You have to think about what cards your opponents need to beat you, what draws are out there, how the flop fits with their preflop action, and possibly what you think your chances are of defending your hand. The point is, start thinking about more than just your own hand. You don't have to be able to break it down to the nth degree like a computer, but you should be more aware of where you stand in the hand.

If I were the above player and I saw this flop, I'd say to myself, "Okay, I don't want to see an 8 or a 10 to complete the inside straight and I don't want to see a king to complete the 9-10-J-Q draw. I'd like you beginners to know that, depending on the number of players and the action on the flop, many good players will actually muck this hand on the flop! It's actually a bad flop if there's a lot of serious interest and raising in the hand. And, with six players and no preflop raise, there's a decent chance that someone has flopped a set, which means that top pair with top kicker is virtually drawing dead.

Beginners also need to know there's a certain kind of flop that they need to be aware of. It's called a *ragged flop*. It simply means a flop where there's no obvious straight or flush draw, and often comes with a high, medium and low card. K♣ 7♥ 2♦ is a perfect example of a ragged flop. This means that with no straight or flush draw, a bettor most likely has a king, and probably with a good kicker. Learn to give credit to the bettor for a decent hand and learn not to chase as often.

This is just a tip from an experienced player: If the betting is capped in a multiway pot on the flop, you probably won't win if all you have is one pair. The cap often represents a flopped set, which means you're drawing dead and don't know it. Just trying to help.

47. FAILING TO PUT A SOLE OPPONENT ON A HAND

As a beginner, no one expects you to be able to read every other player's hand every time. But there's no reason why you can't begin to try! You'll eventually get there with experience, but until then, you can start by just trying to figure out what one player is holding. You should be trying to analyze the play of one player who's in the hand when you're not. And it doesn't have to be boring. You can choose a player who's the biggest winner at the table. You can choose someone you don't like, or you can choose the one player you consider to be the best player at the table. Pick a player based on a criteria that's interesting to you and it will be fun and easier to get a read on his play.

A good place to start learning about putting a player on a hand is when you have A♠ A♥, K♣ K♦ or Q♦ Q♥, and you get it heads-up with another player. When the flop comes, think about every two-card combination he could or should have. Then compare those hands to the cards on the board. You're looking for combinations that could beat you, might beat you, and will beat you.

For example, you have pocket aces, your sole opponent calls a preflop raise and the flop is Q♥ 8♣ 5♦. Unless he flopped a set, you can at this point beat the Q-8, Q-5 and 8-5 combinations.

YOU

BOARD

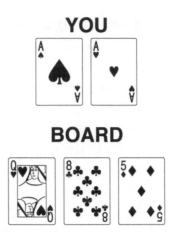

Do you see why?

It's because these are very unlikely holdings for a player who called a raise before the flop. Your pair of aces is likely to still be the best hand at this point.

Turn cards that would pose a threat would be a king (K-Q), another queen (A-Q, K-Q, Q-J), or possibly a 9, 10 or a jack to make the inside straight (J-10, J-9, 10-9). If you can train yourself to learn to do this simple type of logical analysis, you can safely bet a single over-pair on the turn and river more often than the player who doesn't do any thinking.

48. NOT MAKING A CONTINUATION BET ON THE FLOP

Imagine this: Everyone folds around to you on the button and you look down and see A♥ K♥. You raise and both blinds reluctantly call after giving you all the signals that they don't have good hands. The flop is 6♠ 6♦ 2♣.

YOU

BOARD

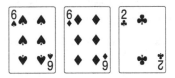

They both check to you. You missed the flop so you check right behind them. You just made a big mistake! Whenever you raise in late position like this you must almost always follow it up with what's called a *continuation bet* on the flop. Your raise before the flop was the first part of a two-part play. You must always act like you have five aces and bet again on the flop. This sells your preflop raise and allows you to win the pot on the flop. Don't make the mistake of not knowing when A♣ K♥ is the best hand. You also have two more cards to come to improve your hand.

There are times when the flop is reasonably threatening and you might want to think about checking, but those times are rare and it takes experience to recognize them. You will win more money in the long run by almost always making continuation bets rather than always being afraid of the flop. Aggression is rewarded in poker. Be the aggressor. Once you've raised, shown aggression, and taken the lead in the hand, the other players will give you a lot of credit for having a good hand. Don't make the mistake of not taking advantage of that fact by not following up with a continuation bet.

49. "CHECK TO THE RAISER"

When a player raises before the flop, it's a good indication that he probably has the best hand at this point and he just might be the leader throughout the hand. So many good things can happen to you when you raise.

1. You win a bigger pot.

2. You buy free cards.

3. You intimidate your opponents.

4. You can set up a future bluff.

5. You can misrepresent your hand.

6. You can induce mistakes from your opponents.

It seems that the biggest mistake the opponents usually make is to check to the raiser when the flop comes, no matter what the flop is. This is a mistake because you are voluntarily giving up too much to the raiser. You're conceding all of the above benefits to the raiser without a fight or an effort to play the hand the way that's best for you.

Anytime I flop a good hand, I will usually go ahead and bet into the preflop raiser if the flop looks like it didn't

exactly fit a raising hand. For example, let's say I have
A♥ 9♥ and the flop is 9♦ 6♣ 3♠.

YOU

BOARD

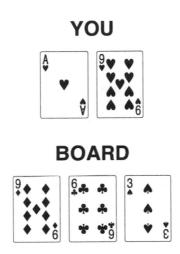

In this situation, I will bet into the raiser. This gives him
a chance to muck two big overcards to make a bad call.
He should also fold pocket eights, sevens, fives, fours
and twos. If he has a pocket pair higher than nines, he
will usually raise and that will help me read his hand. If
I just check and call on the flop because I'm "checking
to the raiser," then I've set myself up to lose chips, or
not win the pot when I had the best hand on the flop.

50. NOT KNOWING THE DIFFERENCE BETWEEN PREFLOP
AND POST-FLOP SKILLS

Preflop skills center around being good at initial hand
selection, playing position and basic hand reading.
Post-flop skills call into play just about all of the other
skills you need at poker: hand-reading, knowing when

to check, bet, call, raise, reraise, slowplay and fold. Most beginners just pick two cards to see the flop with and then go all the way to the river while looking only at their cards and the board. You need to learn to change gears once the flop hits the table.

51. JUST CALLING WITH THE BEST PROBABLE HAND

It doesn't take the nuts to win every hand. The cards that come on the flop determine what the nuts will be and they will always be random cards. You can eliminate the chances of some of your opponents hitting some of these random flops just by raising them out before the flop. Also, you'll usually have an idea if the flop helped others or not. An easy, obvious example would be if you're in a hand with a very tight player who never played a card below a 9 and the flop is 7♣ 4♥ 2♦. In this case, you can be pretty sure that the flop missed your opponent and your A♦ 7♦ is the probable best hand at this point. Use a little deductive reasoning and have the confidence to bet. You will have the best hand most of the time.

52. NOT BETTING STRONG HANDS

Winning poker is all about getting second-best hands to pay off the first best-hands. It doesn't matter if you're playing 7-card stud, draw, or Texas hold'em. The rule is this: Bet when you have the best hand and make the other players pay for the privilege of beating you. Slowplaying and giving free cards are tactics that should seldom be used, particularly when playing low limit against other beginners. They will almost always call anyway because that's what makes them beginners. Let's say you hold A♠ Q♠ and the flop is A♦ Q♣ 7♥.

YOU

BOARD

You should almost always bet and make the straight and flush draws pay to beat you. After all, you're a 5 to 1 favorite over anyone holding K♠ J♦, K♣ 10♥ or J♦ 10♦. They will pay to draw, so why not make them?

Good players will know to fold when you bet a strong hand. However, your typical opponents who are mostly beginners, will almost always call you anyway. Give them a chance to make that mistake.

53. INCORRECT SLOWPLAYING

This is an extension of the above mistake. Slowplaying is deliberately playing a strong hand in a weak manner in order to trap players for future bets. I can tell you that in the typical beginner's game, those players will trap themselves for additional bets without you having to do it for them. The bets that you lose and the free cards you give when you slowplay are too much to give up. As mentioned above, you should always bet your probable best hands, your strong hands, and the nuts. You will get action. The only time that it might be profitable to slowplay is when you have a hand that is insured by the jackpot. In other words, if you lose this hand, you'll hit the jackpot. Under those circumstances, you definitely want someone to catch up with you, but this is a very rare occurrence and should not be a big part of your game.

You have A♦ Q♠. The flop is K♣ J♥ 10♣, giving you the nut straight.

YOU

BOARD

This is the type of hand that you do not have to slowplay because the flop should have also hit your opponents. The difference is that it hit you perfectly while it only merely helped them. You are a huge favorite over any hand they could be drawing to. Make them pay.

54. GIVING TOO MANY FREE CARDS

If you are a beginning player and you don't yet have a lot of experience giving and getting free cards, I want you to know for a fact that giving free cards should not be a tactic in your repertoire right now. You give up too much profit and get too little in return when you're a beginner and you check your strong hands. Giving free cards is an advanced tactic for more experienced players.

55. NOT MAKING DRAWING HANDS PAY

Anytime someone is drawing to a straight or a flush, they will have eight or nine cards available to them if all of their cards are live and they're not drawing dead. That's a couple of big ifs. This means that if you have a hand that can beat a draw, usually a pair or better, then you are a 37 to 8 or 36 to 9 favorite over the other player (we're assuming your opponent has no overcards for additional outs). The fact that he can draw twice — once on the turn and again once on the river — makes you about a 3 to 1 or 4 to 1 favorite to win the hand.

When you've got the best hand at the moment, make the drawing hands pay. Don't slowplay or give free cards. They will pay because:

- They're bad players
- They came to play
- Almost no beginner ever flops a straight or a flush draw and throws it away on the flop; and

- They know that making the draw is the only way they can win the hand

For the rest of your poker playing life, you will win about 70-something percent of these types of hands heads-up. Bet, get money in the pot, and you'll be a big winner in this situation in the long run. But whatever you do, don't slowplay, don't check, and don't try to give free cards. Make them pay!

56. CALLING WHEN YOU SHOULD RAISE

Poker hands after the flop are going to usually fall into one of two types of hands:

1. A pair or better than can win without any or much more improvement, and

2. Hands that are drawing to a straight, a flush, or a longshot specific card.

When you have the made hand, you do not want the drawing hands to beat you. You'd like them to miss their draws while putting more money in the pot for you to win. Often, they will have the correct odds on the flop to draw to the straight or flush. You can usually prevent this by betting or raising on the flop, thereby making the drawing hands call double bets. This usually cuts their pot odds almost in half and makes it correct for them to fold. If they call, then they're making a mistake and you profit from that also. This mistake is simply one of not raising to protect your hand.

57. NOT RESPECTING AN ACE ON THE FLOP

This is a big one. This is huge. That's because an ace comes on the flop about one in four hands, and since it's a key card in any poker game, how you play here has a big impact on your bankroll. Too many beginners lose too much money in this situation and it's a shame because this is one of the easiest leaks in a game that can be fixed. All you have to do is recognize a couple of key facts and then put them together to arrive at a logical conclusion:

A. Many beginners play every time they get an ace; plus

B. When an ace comes on the flop; equals

C. Someone has at least a pair of aces.

It's that easy: A + B = C. All you have to do is assume someone has an ace in his hand to match the one on the board. Yes, I do know what they say about the word assume. This is one time you can profitably bet on an assumption. This statement has some profound, yet simple implications. If you hold K♣ K♦ and the flop is A♠ 9♠ 5♦ and there's a bet, you can safely, confidently and profitably fold your pocket kings in the typical low limit beginner's game. Or, you can play it the other way—always call anyway, and then call again on the turn and river. A player who bets in this spot will have an ace 95 percent of the time. The other times, he will have a set of nines or a set of fives.

The good rule of thumb is this: If you're playing to win with a pair, and you can't beat the aces, let it go. You will be right so often that it's not even a close call that you have to give a second thought to it. Rarely, you will have the best hand with your kings, but you will sometimes lose the hand on the turn or river anyway. Learn to let it go.

In a single eight-hour playing session, there will be an ace on the flop about 60 times! Whenever you have a chance to make the same mistake that many times in one day, you have the potential to lose a lot of money. Look at this as an opportunity to save money in a situation where the other players will not.

To help drive home this very important and costly point, here are a few facts about aces and the flop that you need to know. You cannot be a winner in the long run without knowing these facts and playing accordingly:

- In a ten-handed game, someone will be dealt an ace 87 percent of the time

- If you are dealt an ace in a ten-handed game, someone else will also hold an ace a whopping 75 percent of the time

- In a five-handed game, someone will be dealt an ace 59 percent of the time

- If you are dealt an ace in a five-handed game, someone else will also hold an ace 42 percent of the time

- If you don't have an ace in a five-handed game, someone else will have one about 51 percent of the time

58. PLAYING WHEN THE FLOP IS PAIRED

... and you don't have trips or better. This is another expensive beginner mistake that's easy to fix. If the flop is something like Q♠ 8♦ 8♣ and you don't have the 8♥ or 8♠, then you're in a trap that's going to cost you a lot of money. The problem is not that someone else has an 8, the problem is when you put money in this pot with a losing hand. The first thing that happens is that the player holding A♥ 8♥ is going to check on the flop. This gives you a false sense of security and makes you think that no one has an 8. Your Q♣ J♦ is starting to look pretty good right now, isn't it?

When the innocent-looking turn card comes, you feel pretty good about betting your top pair with a good kicker. That's when you get check-raised for a big bet on the turn or you're raised for an extra bet on the river. This is predictably a losing situation for you. You must be extremely careful when the flop contains a pair.

The two most important factors that you should be aware of are how high is the pair and how many players (that really means total hole cards) are out against you. If the flop is K♠ 2♦ 2♥ and you're heads-up against one player, then a hand other than three deuces is very likely to be good. If the flop is Q♥ Q♦ J♦ with seven-way action, then it's a good chance that someone is holding a queen.

Don't be fooled if everyone checks on the flop because that's just usually how it goes. The number of players who call a bet on the flop is also a good indicator of a queen being out there. If there's a bet and four callers—what can they all possibly have? There are only two other queens left in the deck. The more players there are to call on the flop, the more likely it is that someone would have pocket jacks in this example. Paired flops are trap hands because it allows other players to get way ahead of you on the flop while giving you little chance of catching up. Again, don't be fooled by a check on the flop.

59. PLAYING WHEN THE FLOP IS ALL OF ONE SUIT

... and you don't have one or two cards of that suit. This is an almost identical situation to the above mistake of playing when the flop contains a pair. You can play these flops if you can deduce that you have a reasonable chance to win the pot. The first thing you can do is consider the possibility that no one actually flopped a flush. The odds are always against it, even though it does happen. Just realize that you could be beat with little chance of catching up. You usually need the ace of the flopped suit, or two pair, or a set to call on the flop if there's a bet. Beginners lose a lot of money on these hands because they'll call with second or bottom pair or with a single, low flush card. A good rule of thumb is this: If the flop is better than average, then you need a better than average hand to match it to play. It's that easy. Quit chasing without a reasonable chance to win.

60. PLAYING BACKDOOR DRAWS WITHOUT THE PROPER ODDS

Notice I said, "…without the proper odds." The chances of holding two diamonds, flopping one diamond, and then hitting a diamond on the turn and another one on the river are about 22 to 1 against; they're only fractionally better for a straight draw. Or, if you like, you hold one diamond and flop two diamonds. Either way, you have only three diamonds after the flop and need to hit perfect-perfect on the turn and river. 22 to 1 against equates to roughly 5 percent, which happens to be just about what a one-card out is worth to you after the flop.

So, if you're counting your outs on the flop, and one of them is a backdoor straight or flush draw, you can add one out to the count. It's like flopping a four-flush and having ten more clubs left in the deck instead of only nine. It's not much, but it does add 5 percent to your hand equity and it's worth chasing if the pot is big enough.

If it costs you one small bet on the flop and one big bet on the turn to draw to this backdoor hand, then the final size of the pot needs to be about 30 big bets or more. Then you have to factor in the possibility that you can make your hand and still lose. These types of draws cause big swings in your bankroll because you're going to miss the draw 19 out of 20 times. That's why the pot has to be huge when you make it on your twentieth attempt. In these instances, you should only draw to the nuts.

61. CALLING ON THE FLOP JUST TO PICK UP A POSSIBLE DRAW ON THE TURN

This is an even worse version of trying to make a back-door draw without the proper pot odds. This is all about flopping a three-straight or a three-flush, or both. Say you hold K♠ 10♥ and the flop is J♠ 6♥ 3♥.

YOU

BOARD

You now have three cards to a straight and three cards to a flush. Many beginners with this hand will call in the hopes that the turn card will give them either a four-flush or a four-straight. The odds are about 2 to 1 against the card they need on the turn.

When you're playing like this, you don't know what you're doing and you're leaving your decision-making process up to the turn of a card. That's not the way to play a skillful game of poker. Instead of trying to hit perfect-perfect in a backdoor draw, you're trying to hit lucky-lucky in a game of skill. This should be a very easy mistake to eliminate now that it's been brought to your attention.

62. CALLING ON THE FLOP WITH OVERCARDS ONLY

This is another big, expensive mistake that beginners routinely make. And if the truth be known, too many experienced players make this mistake too often also. Typically, it goes like this: You limp in with K♠ J♦, the flop is 8♥ 5♦ 2♣ and you call a bet on the flop. Wasn't that easy? Any two other high pocket cards and any other three lower flop cards will also serve well in this example.

There will be times when your two overcards happen to make a straight or a flush draw, but that's not what I was talking about here. I'm talking about calling solely in the hopes of pairing one of your hole cards on the turn.

This is a horrible play! There are only 6 of 47 unseen cards that will pair you. You're going to miss 41 times for every 6 times you make a pair. That's about 6 1/2 to 1 against. And then you have to win with the hand. Those are horrendous odds and it's a losing situation in the long run.

Don't make the mistake of thinking that this isn't that important because it isn't at the very beginning of this chapter. It is actually in the top ten of all mistakes in terms of how much it costs in the long run and given how often you have an opportunity to make this mistake. There are times when it's correct to call with A♥ K♠

in this spot, but that will be covered later. Until then, quit calling bets with just overcards.

63. NOT BETTING OVERCARDS ON THE FLOP

Poker is a complicated game and the best way to play any one specific hand depends on how the exact specific action goes down on that hand. As you will learn, the answer to almost any poker question is, "It depends." There will be times when you know two big overcards are the best hand after the flop. The problem is, it takes practice, experience and hand-reading skills to figure this out. Beginners first learn this by accident when they incorrectly call a bet on the flop with nothing but two overcards and they end up catching a bluffer on the river. Sometimes, it's easy to figure out that a bet on the flop is a bluff *while* the bet is being made.

The key is to know the player betting on the flop. If he's a frequent bluffer and bets every time you check to him, you are in a more profitable situation than if he never bluffed. Against a player who never bluffs, you're always going to have to make a hand to win the pot. However, your two big overcards can serve as bluff-catchers against the right players. You just have to know who those players are.

To sum up #62 and #63, above, what I'm saying is that if you hold K♣ Q♣ and the flop is 8♥ 5♠ 2♦, it is much better if you bet first than if you check and call with the same hand.

YOU

BOARD

64. MISPLAYING A♠ K♦ WHEN YOU MISS THE FLOP

This means folding too often as well as calling too often. A♠ K♦ is a big hand, especially before the flop and when played heads-up, or when low cards come on the flop. It is usually seen as a drawing hand and that's probably true when there's seven-way action to see the flop. However, you should learn to think twice before you automatically make the obvious play with it. There will be times when your sole opponent missed the flop and he has A♦ Q♥ or A♥ J♣. Start trying to figure out when it's correct to fold in one situation, but call in another situation with the same hand. This learning can come only from experience, but it is worth working on.

65. CALLING WITH A HOPELESS POCKET PAIR

The flop is A♣ K♦ Q♠ with four callers on the flop. You have 5♥ 5♠. Do you call? The flop is K♦ J♦ 9♦ and you have 8♣ 8♠. Do you call? Take a look at this line of number ones:

1111111111l1111111111111111111l11111111111

Or this line of letter "v"s:

vvvvvvvvvvvvvvvwvvvvvvvvvvvvvwvvvvvvvvvvvvvv

Or this line of letter "c"s:

cccccccecccccccccccccccccccccccccccecccccccccccccc

Did you spot the two letter ls in the line of 1s? Did you spot the two letter ws in the line of vs? And did you see the two letter es in the line of cs? You probably didn't.

These three lines of 47 letters represent the 47 unseen cards left in the deck after you miss your set on the flop. The two letters in each line that don't belong there represent the only two cards that will make you a set. I hope this visual helps illustrate what a longshot it is to make your hand on the turn if you miss on the flop.

If you have a pocket pair and you miss making a set on the flop, then there are only two of the remaining unseen cards that can make you a set on the turn. The odds are 45 to 2 against getting those cards. If you were to turn the two cards you need face-up in the deck, shuffle it, and then spread the deck on the table, it would resemble the three lines of letters above. All of the cards would be face down except for the two cards you need to make a set on the turn. You're just as likely to get the card you need on the turn as you were to have spotted the two odd letters in the above lines. Looks like pretty long odds when you look at it like that, doesn't it? Learn to let those small pocket pairs go when you get big overcards on the flop.

66. RAISING IN EARLY POSITION WHEN YOU'RE ON A DRAW

You have 10♥ 8♥ in the big blind and you see the flop with six other players. The flop is 9♣ 7♦ 3♥.

YOU

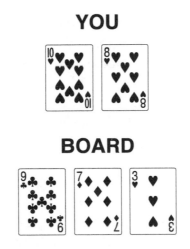

BOARD

The small blind bets first and you're next to act. Do you fold, call or raise? You shouldn't fold because you're going to make a straight one in three times when you're getting 6 to 1 odds. You're definitely going to have to at least call since you're not folding, so the question is: Do you raise? Sadly, too many beginners get so excited over the prospects of this big draw that they incorrectly raise.

Why is raising wrong? Because straight and flush draws require big pot odds to make it mathematically correct to draw to the hand. You *want* as many players as possible in on the hand so you will be compensated for the times you draw to this type of hand and miss. If you raise and knock out the players behind you, you will be paid off by only the small blind when you make your hand. However, if you just call the small blind's bet on the flop, and let everyone in behind you, those players will be in the hand to pay you off when you make the straight.

Notice that this mistake is specific to when you're first to call a bet while on a draw. You lose your customers when you raise. This is not the same as having the same hand on the button and six players have called before the action gets to you. In this situation, you can safely raise to build a pot when you have a positive expectation and you're not likely to drive anyone out.

There's a related mistake that invokes the "Don't raise in early position" rule. It's when you flop the nuts or a monster hand and you're first to call a bet. Just call, so they can call behind you and pay you off. This also applies when you flop a hand that will win the jackpot if you lose the hand. Why drive anyone out when you really need them to stay in the hand and beat you?

67. PLAYING DRAWING HANDS WITHOUT THE PROPER POT ODS

This refers to those times when making the draw is the only way you can win the hand. You need three or four other players in the hand, contributing to the pot all the way just to break even on your draws in the long run.

The problem is that beginners will limp in with hands like Q♠ 8♦, K♥ 2♥, 7♣ 6♣ and J♠ 4♠ when it's obvious there's going to be only two or three players in the hand. You will lose money even when you make the draw because you'll never make enough on your winning hands to make up for the money you put in on your losing hands. You need a lot of players in the pot to play drawing hands.

68. PLAYING GUTSHOT DRAWS WHEN THE POT IS SMALL

The flop is A♠ K♦ 10♥ and you hold Q♣ 6♥, hopefully in the big blind. There's a bet. Do you call, trying to hit the gutshot straight?

YOU

BOARD

The answer depends on the size of the pot. If there's three small bets in the pot, you can't call because you're 11 to 1 to hit it on the next card and you're only getting 3 to 1 or 4 to 1 pot odds. Then, you have to factor in the fact that you might make the straight and have to split the pot. Then there's the possibility that you make the straight and lose the hand anyway. This mistake will be easier to eliminate when you learn more about drawing and pot odds.

69. ALWAYS DRAWING TO THE LOW END OF A STRAIGHT
You hold A♥ 5♥ and the flop is 6♣ 7♦ 8♠.

YOU

BOARD

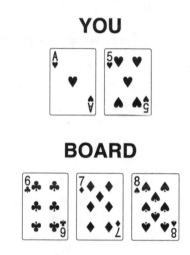

There's a bet. Do you call? I'm telling you that you should fold this hand almost all of the time, even though it looks like an obvious, easy draw. There are several factors at work here that make this a big loser in the long run. Start out with this:

What does the bettor have?

You're undoubtedly already beat at this point. A draw of a 9 is not an out for you because a 10 makes a higher straight. A draw of a 4 makes the straight, but it cuts your pot odds in half if you have to split the pot—and again, you can make the straight and *still* lose. So many things have to happen in the correct order for you to win this hand that you can't possibly show a profit with it in the long run. Drawing to the low end of a straight is called drawing to the sucker or ignorant of the straight. That's not you, is it?

There's another side to this mistake, and it's this: It's sometimes okay to draw to the low end of a straight. If you're able to read your opponents' probable hand, and you know that the card that makes you a small straight won't make him a bigger straight, then you can draw for it if the pot odds justify the draw and you're certain you'll win the hand if you do make the straight. These are questions that take some experience and judgment to answer.

70. NOT FOLDING WHEN THE POT IS SMALL

My students tell me that this is one of the most useful bits of advice I give them. That's because this tip is easy to follow and very valuable to you when you do execute it. Here it is:

If you are truly and genuinely undecided about how to play your hand, then fold when the pot is small.

It doesn't get any easier than that. You have little or nothing invested in the hand, and if you truly are undecided about how to play your hand, then it's because you're being faced with a situation that you're not familiar with. This will happen a lot when you're a beginner. This is not the time to bet you know what you're doing. Fold, watch the hand, try to answer the questions you had about the hand and try to learn something for the next time you're in that same situation. Learn for free.

This does not mean that you should always fold just because the pot is small. What if the flop is J♥ 10♦ 9♣ and there's only $10 in the pot? I'll bet you'd call if you held K♣ Q♣, Q♠ 8♥, J♦ J♠, 10♠ 10♥, or 9♦ 9♥. And you should. Just remember that this advice about small pots applies *only* when you are genuinely undecided between calling and folding.

71. NOT ESTIMATING THE FINAL SIZE OF THE POT

This is another way of figuring out if it's worth it to you to play your hand or not. If you can estimate early on how big the pot is going to be and you can guess how many bets it's going to cost you to play, then you can get a rough idea of your overall odds. If you know the pot is going to be huge, then you might want to voluntarily take the worst of it before the flop with some hands because of the immense implied odds.

Estimating the size of the final pot is not an exact science. It is mostly an assessment of the question, "How big have the recent pots been," and "How likely is it to be nearly as big this hand?" Sometimes, especially in home games or wild public games, the size of the pot is more a function of the looseness of the players rather than the value of the cards. The point is simply that you can see the flop with slightly weaker hands than average if you know it's going to be a big pot before it's all over.

9.
MISTAKES MADE ON THE TURN

72. NOT KNOWING THE BEST TELL OF ALL

There are easily dozens of tells available to you in a low-limit game. There are many that are easy to learn, easy to spot, and easy to take advantage of. All of them are profitable because you get to either save money or get in an extra bet when you spot one or more of these tells. However, there's one tell that's so easy to spot and profit from in a beginner's game that there ought to be a law against it.

What do you think it is?

One of the hallmarks of a beginner's game is that it's full of players who don't know what to do when it's their turn to act. They'll be able to quickly handle the obvious folding, calling and raising situations, but they will have trouble with decisions that are a little more complicated and require more experience than what they have. When confronted with an unfamiliar situation, they will pause, hesitate, delay, deliberate and finally, after much obvious consternation, call. And there you have it! It's called a *hesitation call*.

When a player does not know for sure exactly what he's doing and he reluctantly puts money in the pot, he's just set himself up as a prime target to be attacked and pushed out of the hand on the next betting round. It's a fact that players who make hesitation calls are much more likely to fold on the next betting round if there's a show of strength by an aggressor. There's a time to be just an ordinary opponent, there's a time to be a bettor, and there's a time to be an aggressor. Attack hesitation calls! That means you can bet much weaker hands than usual when you know there's a good chance you won't be called. And even if you are called, you might still win anyway, because his hesitation almost certainly means he has a weak hand. If his was better or worse, he would not have had to hesitate like he did.

The Best Tell of All

Knowing that another player
is truly reluctant to
continue with the hand.

---

73. NOT USING THE DOUBLED BET TO YOUR ADVANTAGE

The turn is when the bets double. This is the time when most players who were happy to call a small bet on the flop will now not want to call a big bet on the turn. Most players who flop an inside straight draw will almost always call a small bet on the flop to try to hit that 11 to 1 longshot. They then intend to fold if they miss because they'll have to call a big bet on the turn, usually without the pot being big enough for them to justify calling. If this is the hand you put your opponent on, then you have to make the big bet on the turn! You also have to bet if you put him on a four-flush drawing hand and the pot is small or he's not getting the right pot odds. This is also the time to bet to force out players with second and third pairs and weak pocket pairs. Do not give free cards if you have any kind of hand at all to protect; make them pay to beat you. A big bet on the turn will help you with that.

74. NOT RAISING WHEN YOU INTEND TO CALL ON BOTH THE TURN AND THE RIVER

This is an extension of the above advice—with a twist. Often you will have a strong hand on the turn that is not the nuts, but it is the probable best hand. Perhaps it's top two pair or a set. If you intend to call a bet on both the turn and the river, you should occasionally put both of those bets in on the turn. That means that you will be raising with hands that you might otherwise usually only call with. The purpose of this is to force out any player who is on a draw that could beat you. Forcing him to call a double bet cold cuts his pot odds in half and will often make it mathematically incorrect for him to call. If he does call, that's alright with you, too.

Since you're going to put two bets into the pot anyway, you can sometimes put them both in at once to cause problems for any callers. Also, if you do happen to improve your hand on the river, or if you otherwise know you have the best hand, you can put another bet in on the river.

75. RAISING FOR THE WRONG REASON

There are five main reasons to raise. They are:

1. To eliminate players.

2. To get a free card.

3. To gain information.

4. To get value from your hand.

5. To bluff.

You make the most money when you raise to eliminate players and when you raise for value. Knocking players out of the hand from the beginning and then getting the remaining players to call extra bets when you have the best hand are the two best uses of a raise.

Raising as a means of bluffing at the pot puts the bettor in a position of either folding his hand or calling just one more bet to see your hand. And, as we all know, he'll most likely always call. It will be a crying call, or a percentage call, but it would be a call nonetheless and you'll still lose the hand. Raising as a pure bluff pretty much works only in pot-limit or no-limit games.

The most overrated reason for raising is to gain information. The information you think you get by having a player call a raise versus a single bet is almost always not worth the extra bet you pay for it. Try it for an entire playing session: resist raising to get information. Determine how many bets you save and ask yourself if the savings was worth it. Did the hand play out about the same way in the absence of that information? I can tell you that most of the time it would have.

The reason is that most players will raise to gain information and then do one of two things:

1. Decide that whatever it is that they think they just learned confirms what they thought they knew anyway. They then proceed on the same original intended course.

2. They learn something new and they still don't change their plan.

You should raise only when you think your raise can show immediate results like:

1. Making players fold.

2. Finding out that opponents want to reraise.

3. Seeing how opponents react given the cards on board.

4. Making opponents check to you on the next round.

5. Making opponents put more money into a pot you expect to win.

6. Giving you information that will change the way you plan to play the hand.

Raising for other reasons is just not a profitable move in the long run.

76. INCORRECT CHECK-RAISING

The reasons to check-raise are:

1. To get more money in the pot.

2. To make players call double bets cold.

3. To trap them for one bet and then another.

4. To force players to fold.

However, you should only check-raise for these reasons when it is mathematically correct to do so and you have the right pot odds. That means you are going to be a big loser in the long run if you check-raise heads-up when the pot is small and you're on a draw. You should not check-raise to drive out players who you know can't win the hand and you shouldn't attempt a check-raise when you're playing against players who won't bet for position or value, or attempt to bluff.

Check-raising is almost always an overused and abused tactic in the hands of average beginners. You should save your check-raising attempts for that once- or twice-per-session time when you're virtually certain it will work. Otherwise, you should bet your hands for value and forget about trying to be deceptive.

77. CALLING RAISES WITH JUST ONE PAIR

The bets double on the turn. With so many different possible hands you can make with four cards on the board, one pair is actually at the bottom of the list of hands you can usually bet comfortably. This means that a bet on the turn usually means that someone has at least a pair or better.

A raise on the turn usually means that if the hand were over on the turn, one pair will usually be the losing hand. As an experienced player, I can tell you that raising contests on the turn are almost never one pair versus one pair affairs. It's usually the raiser (who has two pair or better) raising the bettor (who has only one pair).

Your job, as a spectator and then as a potential caller, is to know this in advance and avoid calling these players when you hold only one pair.

There are two possible exceptions to this guideline:

1. When you hold A♦ A♥ and, in your opinion, the river card could give you a better two pair (or a better hand).

2. You hold a pocket pair higher than the highest card on the board and you think the river card will give you a winning hand.

If you have one pair on the turn and there's some raising going on, you should carefully evaluate the hand and figure out if your opponent could be raising with less than what you have. Most of the time the answer will be no and you should be able to see that you're beat and you should muck the hand.

78. TELEGRAPHING SERIOUSNESS

If you're going to take their money, you really do need them to like you. Nobody likes to lose to someone who makes it obvious that the only thing he's interested in is your money. This is not high on the list of beginner mistakes. Most beginners are happy, playful, cheerful, talkative and outgoing. It's only as they get better as a player and start to take the game more seriously do they change demeanors. The fact is that other players give more action to opponents they like than to opponents they don't like.

Don't forget to smile, be polite, congratulate someone when they beat you in a hand, and rejoice in their triumphs. Besides being the right thing to do, you'll make more money in the long run.

79. EDUCATING PLAYERS AT THE TABLE

I'll bet you can recognize each one of the following scenarios from your actual live play:

A. Everyone limps before the flop. The board is Q♠ J♥ 10♦ 5♣ 2♠ and the player in last position turns over A♦ K♦ for the nuts and wins a big pot. How many times have you heard someone ask, "You had A-K and didn't raise before the flop?"

B. It's heads-up on the river. The first player bets the instant the river card hits the table. The second player calls with a pair of threes and wins the pot. And then he says, "I knew you were bluffing. You bet it out too fast. If you had made a hand, you'd have needed a few seconds to think about it."

C. Four players see the river card. The board is Q♦ J♥ 10♦ 5♠ 2♦. The player in last position turns over A♦ K♦ and wins the pot with the nut flush. And then one of the other players says, "You had A-K suited and you didn't raise?"

D. The first player under the gun raises before the flop. Six players call. The board is Q♠ J♥ 6♠ 2♥ 10♦ and the first player to call the preflop raise wins the pot when he shows 9♦ 8♦ for a straight. Whereupon, the preflop raiser says in a high-pitched whine, "You called a raise with that in early position?"

E. Only the blinds call to see the flop. The flop is K♣ 7♥ 5♦. The small blind checks and calls. The turn is the A♦. He checks and calls again. The river is the 4♠ and the small blind now bets and is called. He shows a 6♦ 3♥ for a straight and wins the hand. The player in the big blind then says, "You drew to a gutshot straight heads-up and with no money in the pot?"

F. The board is K♥ J♥ 8♥ 5♥ 4♥ and the first player bets into his only opponent. That player folds and the bettor graciously shows A♣ A♠. The player on his right then leans over and whispers to him, "You shouldn't have bet that—you're only going to get called if you're beat."

G. You have 10♠ 8♠ in the big blind. The board is J♦ 9♦ 7♣ 5♠. You and your only opponent raise and reraise each other four times, and then just to be sure, you raise one last time. He just calls that fifth raise. The river is the 2♣. He bets into you and because of the action on the river, you save time by just calling, expecting to split the pot. You win the hand with the nuts. Then he shows you J♣ J♠ and says, "Thanks, but why did you stop raising on the river? You had nothing to lose."

H. A new player joins the game. On the next hand, he's the only player to call a preflop raise and he loses a big pot. After the hand is over, the player sitting next to him leans over and says, "I guess you didn't know that that player only raises before the flop with pocket aces or kings."

I. There are three players at the river. The river card makes a straight and a flush very likely. The first player bets and is called by the second player. The third player calls. The first player made the flush, the second player made the straight and the third player had only middle pair with a good kicker. After the hand, the second player said to the third player, "How could you call with almost nothing? Even though the first bettor could have been totally bluffing, I had to have had a hand good enough to call him and to withstand a possible raise from you."

J. And then there's the Poker Professor, the one player at every table who autopsies and analyzes the play of every hand. He provides a nonstop commentary—a never ending motormouth who tells you everything he knows about how to play every hand.

The point is obvious—the game is all about knowing things and having strengths and abilities that your opponents don't. That's how you take their money. Why would you want to sabotage yourself? On the other hand, you can get educated just by asking for an opinion. You're not going to tell them anything, but there's certainly no law that says they can't educate you. All you have to do is ask the player sitting next to you how he would have played that hand or what he thinks the other player is holding. Some people will tell you everything they know. Or think they know.

80. EMBARRASSING PLAYERS INTO EITHER PLAYING BETTER OR LEAVING THE GAME

This is an extension of the above mistake. The new mistake is that in addition to telling another player how to play better, you do it in a way that's insulting, hurtful, condescending and perhaps just plain brutally honest. When you criticize another's quality of play in such a way that you hold him up for ridicule in front of his fellow players, it cannot possibly end in a good result for you. No one responds favorably to rude behavior. The player you've victimized will react to you and it will almost always be in a way that will cost you money in the long run.

He will probably stop giving you action, unless he's very sure he has your hand dominated. You might be set up for an unexpected check-raise. You might have to endure hearing an ugly comment yourself when you lose a hand. And lastly, and most likely, your new enemy will probably just start playing as well as he knows how to against you. Most players don't play their best game all the time, but one sure way to force them to is to embarrass them into it.

81. NOT FOLDING GREAT-LOOKING, BUT SECOND-BEST, HANDS

This is a hard one for beginners because mastering this one marks an important turning point in the education of beginning poker players. This is where a beginner needs enough experience and confidence in his own ability that he is able to sort through all of the good and correct advice to arrive at a correct decision. The problem is that the strategy advice loses specificity and becomes contradictory as you get further into the hand. You might ask yourself these questions when you're in a tough situation:

- Should I fold because I think my opponent has me beat, or should I call because the pot is big?

- Should I bet because I just made my straight, or should I check and fold because the board has four hearts and there are two callers?

- Should I do this or that? Should I fold, call or raise?

A beginner who asks himself these questions is well on his way to becoming a winner once he gains enough experience to be able to throw away a good-looking but second-best hand on the turn.

I specifically remember that I turned that corner when I was playing $10/$20 hold'em at the Stardust in 1985. I held A♠ 10♠ and the board was K♠ 8♠ 5♠ 8♥.

ME

BOARD

The action went bet-raise, raise and reraise before it got to me. Three other players were going to put $80 into the pot while *I* held the nut flush. I just knew there was a full house out there and when the action got to me, I said, "Okay, I hate to let this go, but I'm going to let my head rule my heart and listen to these players. They're telling me that one of them has a full house. I just don't see all of this action happening if all they have is the second-nut flush."

So, I let the hand go. King's full won the hand and was I ever so proud of myself. I sat there for a moment in silence and let the lesson sink in. I knew I had just graduated to the next grade in poker school.

10.
MISTAKES MADE ON
THE RIVER

82. NOT BETTING WHEN YOU'VE BEEN LEADING THROUGH-OUT THE HAND

This happens most often when you start with two big cards, you get a good draw, bet the flop and turn, and you miss on the river. What you need to understand is that many times your opponents will call you on the flop with the intention of folding on the river if they don't make their hands. Most of the time that you're first to bet, it's because you have a good pair or a hand that's worth protecting against draws. Sometimes, however, you might be betting with a draw that has a lot of outs and you're just betting on making it this time. If you miss by the river and don't bet, then you've just delivered the boxing 1-2 punch without the 2.

A bet on the flop conveys strength. A bet on the turn conveys more strength. A bet on the river says, "I have the winner." Other players will fold when you say you have the winner—just don't forget to say you have the winner.

83. NOT BETTING WHEN YOU MAKE YOUR HAND

This mistake refers to the generally true adage that beginning players usually pretend to be weak when strong, and pretend to be strong when weak. A player who survives the flop and turn and makes his hand on the river is usually pleasantly surprised. His first reaction is to try to hide his newfound hidden strength so that he can maximize his profit and possibly check-raise. This means that a player on a good straight or flush draw will bet or call on the flop and the turn, and then check on the river when he makes the straight or flush. It's an automatic (and understandable) reflex on the part of beginners, but it's almost always the wrong thing to do.

When you've been betting and drawing to a hand, you should almost always bet that hand right out when you make it on the river. That's because of the likelihood that if you check when the possible straight or flush card comes on the river, everyone else will too.

Let's say the board is:

BOARD

The A♣ represents the very real possibility of a made straight or flush, or even both. Q♦ J♥ is a very possible holding for someone, as well as two clubs. You need to bet so you can be paid off by the second-best hands and anyone who wants to play the role of bluff catcher.

84. NOT BETTING WHEN YOU INTEND TO CHECK AND CALL ANYWAY

This applies most when there's just the two of you on the river, or there are several of you in the hand and no one bet the flop or turn. Often, all the players will have high cards and the board will contain only low cards.

If two or more players have (nearly) identical hands, then who wins the hand?

The more aggressive player.

Let's say you have K♦ J♠, your opponents hold A♣ 10♠, Q♦ 9♥ and J♥ 10♦, and the board is 8♠ 6♥ 4♦ 2♣ 8♦.

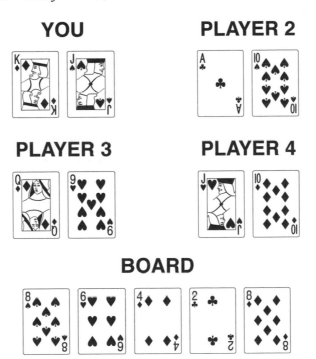

YOU

PLAYER 2

PLAYER 3

PLAYER 4

BOARD

Who wins the hand? The first player to bet at the pot. If you intend to check and call because you know you can beat a bluff, you will win much more often if you bet it right out yourself.

You hold A♥ Q♥ and the board is A♦ J♠ 7♣ 4♦ 7♥.

YOU

BOARD

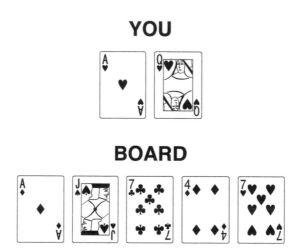

You bet on the flop and the turn, and now the 7♥ means your opponent could have just made trip sevens to beat you. You plan to check and call just in case. This is usually wrong. The reason is that the 7♥ looks just as scary to him as it does to you if he doesn't have it. He most likely has an ace with a weaker kicker. You should bet and expect to get paid off with a crying call. This is a situation where only experience can teach you that it's safe to bet a mediocre hand for value. Beginners should start to think about these check and call situations because they are really bet-for-value situations in disguise.

85. NOT KNOWING WHEN YOU'RE BEAT

Before you start to think I'm being too tough on you, I want to assure you that world-class, superstar champions play hands all the time where they don't know they're beat. Unless you win every single hand you're ever going to play for the rest of your life, you're always going to be beat your fair share of the time. The mistake is in not starting to think about when those times might be and starting to try to read hands and compare the other players' hands to your own.

Beginners like to play any two cards and then call to the end if they make a pair or better. It's fun to play that way, and yes, you will sometimes catch a bluff on the river, but it's a style of play that guarantees you'll lose your buy-in very quickly.

After all the cards are out, you have to learn to pause for a moment while you add up all the information you've collected and try to arrive at a conclusion as to what your opponents might have. Granted, it takes time and experience to hone this skill. You will call many times on the river with losing hands because you didn't know you were beat. Your goal is to start to think about those calls, recognize common, recurring situations where your hand is no good and start to save money by folding when you're beat. It's okay to call and lose if you think you have any chance to win. The mistake is not thinking about the situation at all.

86. NOT GIVING YOUR OPPONENTS ENOUGH CREDIT

This is related to the above mistake, but it's not the same thing. There are many, many reasons why most players are overall losers at hold'em. No one is a big loser for just one reason. All of these mistakes are interrelated to some degree. Often, it's impossible to make just one mistake. Here's one way to look at a unifying theory of mistakes:

Why do you lose at poker?
Because you put money into pots that you don't win. (That kinda says it all, doesn't it?)

Why do you do that?
Because you don't realize that you're going to lose the hand.

Why is that?
Because you don't give your opponents enough credit for possibly holding a better hand than you do.

What can I do about that?
You have to learn how to make progressively better and better laydowns. Quit making loose calls. Quit calling with nothing, hoping to pick up a draw on the turn. Respect position and raises. And realize that the greater the number of players there are in the hand, the better the final hand will be.

For example, if there's a four-straight and a four-flush on the board, the number of players in the hand is your most important consideration. Five opponents means there are 10 cards out against you to make the hand. You have to give credit in situations like this.

It's been said that the beginning of wisdom is the acknowledgement that you don't know everything. Try working with the fact that your opponents often know more than you do.

87. ASSUMING YOU HAVE A SPLIT POT

You have K♦ 10♣ and the board is A♥ Q♠ J♦ 7♣ 5♠. Your opponent bets into you and you just call.

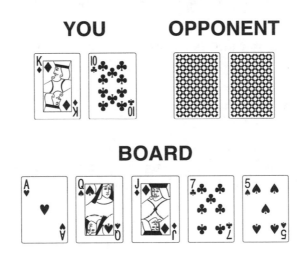

YOU   **OPPONENT**

BOARD

You have K♦ 10♣ and the board is K♠ 8♠ 5♥ 8♦ K♥. Your opponent bets into you and you just call.

YOU   OPPONENT

BOARD

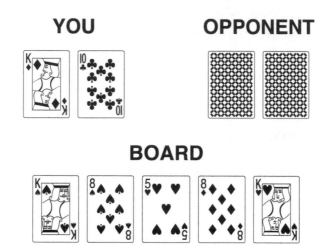

Just calling is a mistake in both of these examples. Your opponent could be betting because he could have two pair, trips, a smaller straight, a full house, or he could just be outright bluffing.

You have absolutely nothing to lose and everything to gain by raising and reraising every time you have the nuts. This is a situation where you will be a winner in the long run because you will always get maximum value out of your nut hands while other players, in the same situation, will charge you only one bet. They will be losers in this spot because they will assume they have a split pot. Don't be that loser.

Let's say your opponent has the nut straight, as in the above example, and you have trip aces. Now, you don't know for a fact that he has the straight. As a matter of fact, he has to be holding exactly K-10 to beat you.

But you decide to bet into the pot for value. What if your opponent assumes you have the straight and he just calls, expecting to split the pot? Well, he just made a mistake, didn't he? His assumption saved you from having to make a crying call with a losing hand.

This should easily be one of those mistakes that you will never make. Let the other players make assumptions and lose bets.

Never assume! Don't play to split—play to win!

88. NOT RECOGNIZING PLAY-THE-BOARD HANDS

Sometimes you can get so wrapped up in playing your hand that you might miss the big picture at the river. You have A♥ 5♥ and the flop is A♣ 5♦ K♥. You just flopped two pair. The turn is the K♠ and the river is the Q♦. Your opponent shows A♣ 10♠ and you see right away that his kicker beats yours. A lot of beginners will mistakenly muck their hand and say, "Nice hand."

YOU   **OPPONENT**

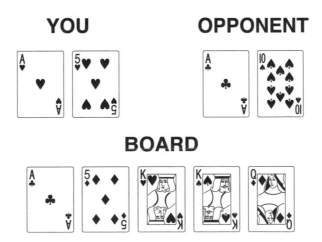

BOARD

That's a mistake! You both have two pair—aces and kings with a queen kicker. It's a split pot. Always double-check your hand and if you have any doubt at all, turn it face-up for the dealer to read.

89. BLUFFING FOR NO REASON IN PARTICULAR

This is a beginner's favorite. Bluffing is okay. Bluffing and losing is okay. As a matter of fact, most bluff attempts are unsuccessful. The mistake is in not thinking about the factors that make a bluff attempt successful. Certain things have to be in your favor or you are just throwing your money away. Bluffing is covered in another chapter, but there is one aspect that is worth looking into and repeating.

If you know absolutely nothing about bluffing, you should at least know this: The more players you bluff into, the worse the math gets for you. Let's look at it two different ways:

First, assume you're going to try to run a bluff through five players. Further assume that it's equally likely that each player will either call or fold. That gives you a formula of $1/2 \times 1/2 \times 1/2 \times 1/2 \times 1/2 = 1/32$ or 31 to 1 against. The pot has to be offering you 31 to 1 odds just have a chance to break even in the long run. The last player will almost always call you with *anything* to keep you from winning a pot that big with only one bet.

Second, assume that there's a better than 50-50 chance that each player will call you. Let's make it a small increase of only 10 percent, meaning there's a 60 percent chance each player will call you. Now, your formula looks like this: 3/5 x 3/5 x 3/5 x 3/5 x 3/5 = 128 to 1. Save your bluff attempts for only one or two other players. A slight increase of only 10 percent that each player will call you raises your chances from 31 to 1 to 128 to 1. Imagine what your chances of success would be if there was a 75 percent chance that each player would call you! (It's 1,024 to 1.)

90. JUST CALLING WHEN YOU MAKE THE NUTS

I know what you're thinking when you make the nuts and just call when a player bets. You're hoping someone behind you will raise so you can reraise and trap everyone for an extra bet. The problem is that when the river card comes and the nuts is very obvious—and the cards that it takes to make the nuts are a rational holding—it tends to kill the action. Everybody is afraid of the nuts when they don't have it themselves.

So, unless you have some concrete, specific reason to believe that there'll be a bet on your immediate left, then you should usually just go ahead and raise and let the chips fall where they will. You will make more money in the long run by playing your hand the obvious way than if you try to get sneaky. One of the things that makes beginners bad players is that they will more likely call your double bet than they will fall for a trick check-raise.

You should almost never just call when you make the nuts.

91. CHECKING STRAIGHT FLUSHES AND FOUR OF A KINDS

In 1985, I was in a hold'em game with Amarillo Slim Preston. I made four fives on the river and checked it to him. He checked right behind me. When I showed him my hand he said, "Son, there's something you just don't understand about poker." His comment has always stuck with me, even though I think he was only about 90 percent right about the way I played that hand.

The point is, I've learned that you'll make a lot more money by being raised when you have a big hand like that than you will by trying to check-raise with it. Always bet your four of a kinds and straight flushes. At least you'll win one bet and possibly a lot more. But you have to start the action; you can't count on anyone else betting your hand for you.

If you bet with a straight flush, you might get some crying calls from players with a weaker flush, two pair or a straight. One of them might even raise to represent the straight flush himself! Then you can reraise. That's how you get money in the pot. You are much more likely to get a bet or two in the pot by betting than you are by trying to check-raise.

92. NOT CALLING WHEN THE POT IS HUGE

I don't mean you should always call when the pot is huge. Sometimes, considering your hand, it would be an obviously stupid thing to do. I'm talking about those times when you have somewhat of a hand on the river and you are genuinely and truly undecided between calling and folding. In cases like this, you must almost always lean toward calling. But let me say it again—that's if, and only if, you really can't figure out what the best course of action is. Let calling be your default move in this spot.

There are several good reasons for calling when you're not sure of what else to do. Folding will cost you a big pot. Calling and losing will only cost you one bet. Calling and winning is hugely profitable. There's a reason you have genuine doubt that keeps you from automatically and easily folding. Sometimes that reason is hard to articulate, but you feel it in your gut. Settle the issue by refusing to let a big pot go for only one bet when you have good reason to second guess yourself if you fold. Treat yourself to the pleasure of knowing for sure. You'll be pleasantly surprised many times.

93. CALLING WHEN THE POT IS SMALL

When the pot is very small, it is usually because there's only two of you in the hand. Since straight and flush draws require 2 to 1 odds and you're only getting 1 to 1, it makes most hands unplayable. You're going to have to rely on winning with two high cards. When the pot is small, you have little incentive to chase with a weak hand and you're just risking too much to get back too little when you do win.

However, realize that the mistake here is calling and not betting when the pot is small. If you're first to bet heads-up, your opponent should correctly fold most of the time. Let them be the one to make this mistake, not you.

There is one easily recognizable, very common situation that occurs on the flop where you — the average beginning player — can plug a big leak in your game starting right now. That is when you flop an open-end or a gutshot straight draw. Almost every player on the planet will automatically say to himself, "Okay, I'll take one off (see the turn card) and if I miss, I'll either check or fold rather than call a big bet on the turn."

You're 2 to 1 to hit the open-ender and 11 to 1 to hit the gutshot. Even though you might see it as a reasonable close call, I can assure you that you'll save a ton of money in the long run if you never call that first bet on the flop heads-up. The math just doesn't support that draw when the pot is very small. Save those chips for when you can get 3 to 1 or better with them.

Elephants can have fleas but fleas can't have elephants. If you're constantly throwing elephant-sized bets at flea-sized pots, you're not going to win the battle of the drain on your bankroll. The constant drain of gambling big on small pots is not something that the average beginner can do. Avoid that situation.

94. NOT PAUSING AFTER CALLING A LIKELY BLUFF
…if you think that the bet you just called on the river was a likely bluff. Some bluffers will realize that they are beat when called on the river and rather than face

the embarrassment of having to show a bluff, will muck their hand without wanting to show it. Give your opponent time to muck his hand. Remember, you didn't call because you knew you had him beat, you called because you knew he'd muck his hand if you called. All you have to do is be patient and give him time to muck his hand so that when the board is K♣ J♥ 8♦ 4♦ A♠, you won't have to show that you called him down on the river with 10♥ 9♠!

Always give a bluffer time to save face.

95. NOT RECOGNIZING ABANDONED POTS

Many times during a playing session, no one will flop a hand worth betting or bluffing with and all they want to do is get the hand over with so they can go on to the next one. Everyone will check on the flop, turn and river, and it will be apparent that the first bettor will force everyone to fold and he will win the pot. Work at recognizing these situations and then develop the courage to pick up the pot with a bet, regardless of your hole cards. I promise, other players are stealing pots from you in this situation and you probably don't realize it. It's your duty to return the favor.

96. NOT ASKING YOURSELF, "WHY DID I LOSE THAT HAND?"

There are many legitimate reasons why you can lose a hand. Some of them are just out of your realm of control. And some are not. A quick review of this list of mistakes will help you figure out where you might have gone wrong.

Have you ever seen Tiger Woods miss a putt? Rarely, but when it does happen he just doesn't walk away or move on to the next hole. He stands there going over the swing in his mind. He figures out what went wrong so he won't make the same mistake on that hole again.

When everybody else at the table is laughing, having fun and raking in that pot you just lost, ask yourself, "Why did I lose that hand?"

97. OVERUSING THE RIGHT TO SEE A HAND

There's a rule in every cardroom in the country that says if a hand is called on the river, then any player at the table has a right to see the called hand. It's a good rule because its purpose is to aid in the prevention of collusion.

Very often, there will only be two players left at the river. One will bet, the other will call, and when he sees he has a loser, muck his hand. It's very natural for you to want to see what he called with, especially if you're a good player and you've been following the action. It's okay to say something like, "Gee, I sure would like to see what you had," whereupon the dealer will kill his hand and turn it face up for everyone to see.

The mistake occurs when you try to use this right to see called hands for purposes other than a natural, friendly curiosity. Some players will pick on a certain player and ask to see every one of his called hands. This is targeting a player for embarrassment and ridicule. It goes against the spirit of the rule and is a rude thing to do.

What happens next is that the targeted player will start playing better, he'll pick better starting hands, and he'll play more carefully, especially when playing a pot against his nemesis. I'm sure you can see why you'd not want to abuse the right to see a called hand—it just costs you money in the long run.

There a related flip side to this mistake and that's when a player voluntarily shows his hand after winning the pot when he did not have to. There's no good reason for this. You're giving away too much information for free when you do that. If you're really proud of your winning hand and you have to boast, then tell them what you had without showing your cards. That way, you get the satisfaction of bragging about how well you played without actually having to prove it.

98. STAYING IN A BAD SEAT

There are many factors that could exist than would make you feel like you're sitting in a bad seat. What they all have in common is that they will all cost you money in the long run.

Here's a sample list:

REASONS TO CHANGE YOUR SEAT

a. #1 or #10 seat—you've got the dealer's box whacking your knee and your personal space is being squeezed by the dealer and the player on your left/right.

b. You're in the #2, #3, #4, #7, #8 or #9 seat, and you're too far away from the flop to see the cards.

c. Your seat is directly in the path of an air conditioning unit or heater.

d. You're seated next to a smoker, a non-bather or a motormouth.

e. The player on your right keeps raising before the flop.

f. The player on your left keeps raising before the flop.

g. The player on your right check-raises you all the time.

h. The player who "has your number" is on your left.

The list could go on and on. The point is, you're making a mistake if you don't do something about it. I know it's difficult to move out of a seat you're physically comfortable in, but poker is not about comfort—it's about making good decisions. (You thought I was going to say it's about making money, didn't you?)

If you're in a seat you don't like for some reason, and you don't do anything about it, you're the one making the mistake.

99. STAYING IN A BAD GAME

Often, the same things that make for a bad seat also make for a bad game. Sometimes things are so bad that changing seats only has the same effect as rearranging the chairs on the deck of the Titanic. If you realize that the table you're at is just a modern day version of the Titanic—then get off that ship! More than a thousand original "players" made it off the real Titanic, so there's hope for you too.

The thing that makes it hard to change tables is that it's a lot more complicated than just changing seats. You actually have to go back up the podium and get your name on a Seat Change List. Then you have to watch your progress on the list and make sure they don't overlook you at the opportune time, which they are likely to do. That's a lot of work! It takes a lot of effort to change tables and that's why you don't see too many beginners do it. But if you're sitting there playing hand after hand, knowing you'd rather not be at that table, you're making a big mistake.

100. COMPLAINING ABOUT BAD LUCK

There's not one single positive thing that can come out of complaining about your bad luck. Every time you complain, all you're really saying is, "I'm a victim, pick on me some more." Complaining emboldens your opponents and encourages them to take shots at you. It promotes a gang mentality against you and ensures that you stay the worst player in the game. In all my years of playing, I've never seen a whiner be a winner. Well, maybe Phil Hellmuth, but he's a special case and he just proves there's an exception for every rule.

If you're a beginner and you're complaining about your bad luck, it's probably because you're more of a beginner than you realize or want to admit. There's also the very real possibility that poker is just not for you. No one wins every hand and it take hundreds, or thousands, of hands for the long-term odds to start to average out. Poker is played for the long haul — that means starting now and going to the end of your life — and beginners just have to accept that fact. Complaining is a mistake that actually costs you money in the long run.

101. OVERTIPPING

Every time you win a hand, money is taken from you! Have you ever looked at it like that? The rake, the jackpot drop, and the dealer's toke all come out of the winner's pot. It can be as much as a full big bet or even more.

The only one of the three factors you can control is the dealer's tip. Everyone rightfully has their own idea of how much to tip for a winning hand. My personal philosophy is that no tip should exceed $1 in your typical $2/$4 or $3/$6 hold'em game, except for that once-a-day monster sized pot, in which case I'd tip $2. You can save a lot of tip money if you start to look at the pots you win with an eye toward exactly how much of that pot is profit to you. I don't tip when the pot is about $19 or less because as much as one-half of that pot could be your money to begin with and a tip could represent 10 percent or more of your win.

Most beginners tend to play too many hands, win too many pots, and tip too much. I've seen players buy-in for $100, tip as much as $75 in a few hours and then quickly go home broke. They tipped themselves out of the game! That's a mistake.

11.
MISTAKES MADE
AFTER THE GAME

Mistakes made after the game? You didn't know these were possible, did you? Well, read on.

102. NOT ASKING FOR A DINNER OR HOTEL ROOM COMP IF YOU'RE PLAYING IN A CASINO POKER ROOM

The rake is taken out of every pot to cover the cost of doing business. Giving you a dinner or room comp is one of those costs of doing business. They actually set aside part of that rake to give back to the players in the form of comps. You've paid for it, don't be bashful about asking for it. They expect you to and they're ready for your request.

Some poker rooms require you to get a poker room player's card and swipe in and out to keep track of your hours of play. You're then awarded a certain amount of money per hour (usually $1 per hour) for playing and you can use it whenever you want to. It's like free money and it's a mistake not to take advantage of it.

103. NOT REVIEWING YOUR OWN PLAY FOR OBVIOUS MISTAKES RIGHT AFTER THE GAME

Why don't you take the time to write down your one or two biggest mistakes of the night right after you get out of the game? Then, review this chapter. If that's all you ever do in this regard, then you'll be ahead of 95 percent of the other players and you will make faster progress as a poker player (that means making fewer mistakes) than the other guys.

104. NOT THINKING ABOUT YOUR OPPONENTS' MISTAKES

All you have to do is look for them during the play of the hand, think about the mistake they made, make sure you know how to not make that mistake yourself, and then go on to the next hand. You will often have to wait until the hand is over to see what the players had, but you can do it. This exercise serves as a good, positive reinforcement — about once every two minutes.

105. NOT FINDING ONE ASPECT OF YOUR GAME TO WORK ON FOR THE NEXT TIME YOU PLAY

You might not have known that this was expected of you. You're going to have to make this a regular part of your post-game autopsy if you're going to make progress as a poker player. There's an exercise at the end of this chapter that will help you with that.

106. NOT TAKING BASIC NOTES

In my *Big Book of Poker,* I wrote a chapter on taking notes where I listed as many as forty factors you could record after each playing session. Who's that obsessive-compulsive? Not me. I don't even take that many notes myself. If you can just keep track of where you played, how many hours you played, a few narrative remarks and what your win/loss was, you'll be doing just fine. Mainly, all you really want to know is what your hourly rate is in terms of big bets.

The reason that this is so important is that there's a *huge* difference between not taking any notes at all and taking the one minute that it requires to keep absolute minimum records. Surveys have revealed that winners take notes and losers don't. I think it has something to do with denial. Don't be a loser—take some notes.

107. NOT TALKING WITH OTHER POKER PLAYERS ABOUT THE GAME OR WHAT THEY THINK OF YOUR ABILITIES

If you're still a rank beginner, then you're not really making that big a mistake if you don't consult with other poker players. That's because you still have so much to learn that other players might fill you with information overload. You can't do everything at once! At this juncture in your poker career, all you have to do to avoid this mistake is read a few poker books and magazines. It's the same thing as having a pro talk directly to you, except it's a one-sided conversation. But that's alright—it's about all you need at this point. But give some thought to reaching out to your fellow players when you can. Hey—send me an email question if you like.

108. NOT PROTECTING YOUR POKER PLAYING BANKROLL

This might be one of the most difficult mistakes of all to avoid making. It's hard for the average beginner to be able to put away $500 or $3,000 just for poker playing. This is especially true if you're married and have a lot of financial obligations. The mistake is in not trying, if poker is going to be a big part of your life. You could do anything—from keeping your wad of poker-playing cash in a separate pocket to having a checking account devoted exclusively to poker. You just have to try to figure out what will work for you.

109. NOT RESEARCHING THE ANSWERS TO SPECIFIC QUESTIONS THAT CAME UP IN YOUR MIND DURING THE GAME

This goes with keeping basic notes after the game. Try to find one thing about hold'em that you don't know every time you play. Then try to find the answer to that question before the next time you play. Players who think about poker when they're away from the table will be winners. Try to join that club.

I saved the last two mistakes for your personal input.

110. TOP TROUBLE SPOTS

For this mistake, I want you to write the number (or numbers) of one or more of the above mistakes that you feel you have the most trouble overcoming. This will help you focus on the one mistake that you feel will be the most beneficial for you to eliminate. When you feel that you've conquered this one worst mistake, replace it with the one that you most want to work on next. Repeat until you've completed the homework assignment below.

111. MISTAKES NOT COVERED HERE

I'd like you to write in any mistake or comment that you can think of that's not covered in this chapter. I'm sure I didn't get 'em all.

_____

_____

_____

_____

_____

_____

_____

_____

_____

_____

_____

12.
THE TOP 10 MOST COSTLY MISTAKES

Not all mistakes are created equal. How much a mistake might cost you depends on how often you get a chance to make it and how certain it is you'll put your money in the pot when you shouldn't. What follows is a list of the top 10 most costly beginner mistakes. The mistakes listed in the previous chapters were in the chronological order that they occur during the play of a hold'em hand. They were not listed in the order of most costly to least costly.

For that reason, I've gone through the list and determined which 10 mistakes are costing you the most money right now. If you didn't win the last time you played hold'em, it was probably because the top 10 kept you down. Here's my list of the most costly mistakes, and, therefore, the ones that you should work in immediately.

9. Incorrect Starting Hand Selection

18. Playing Too Many Hands

57. Not Respecting an Ace on the Flop

35. Calling Too Loosely in the Small Blind

31. Cold Calling Preflop Raises

62. Calling on the Flop With Overcards Only

37. Overdefending Your Big Blind

51. Just Calling With the Probable Best Hand

58. Playing When the Flop is Paired

3. Minimizing Mistakes

If you'll make learning and correcting these mistakes your first priority, you'll instantly save a lot of money and it will help keep you from busting out of the game while you're learning and improving on other aspects of the game. If you can conquer this Top 10 List, you should have immediate and easily recognizable positive results.

HOMEWORK ASSIGNMENT

The numbers 1 to 109 below represent each one of the mistakes beginners make that were listed in the previous chapters. Your assignment is simply to black out each number as you learn about it and then learn to not commit each mistake. Make sure you have completely learned the lesson by heart, totally conquered the mistake, and know that you'll never commit that mistake again in the future. There's no time schedule or time limit—it's up to you to work at your own pace. Good luck!

1	2	3	4	5	6	7	8	9	10
11	12	13	14	15	16	17	18	19	20
21	22	23	24	25	26	27	28	29	30
31	32	33	34	35	36	37	38	38	40
41	42	43	44	45	46	47	48	49	50
51	52	53	54	55	56	57	58	59	60
61	62	63	64	65	66	67	68	69	70
71	72	73	74	75	76	77	78	79	80
81	82	83	84	85	86	87	88	89	90
91	92	93	94	95	96	97	98	99	100
101	102	103	104	105	106	107	108	109	110

If you can think of any additional mistakes that should be added for future editions, please send me a note. I welcome hearing from you.

13.
KEN WARREN ANSWERS YOUR QUESTIONS

I've received thousands of emails since I published my personal email address (kennolga@yahoo.com) in earlier books. I'm glad I could help most of my readers with their poker questions, and in the process I learned a lot myself. Also, in the process, I came to realize that there are many different aspects to poker. Not everything there is to know fits easily and neatly into nicely segregated chapters. There's a lot of poker information left over that just doesn't fit into the overall scheme of an instructional-style book.

So, here it is, a miscellaneous chapter that's a collection of the best of the best email questions I've received. I made sure that each one is interesting and relevant.

ACE-QUEEN (A-Q)
Why does A-Q have such a bad rap? After all, it is two of the three highest cards you can get. How can that be bad?
The bad talk about A-Q started fifty years ago among the no-limit road gamblers of Texas and the Southern circuit—and for good reason. A big preflop raise in these games often meant that the raiser had either an A♠ A♣, K♥ K♦ or A♦ K♠ —all hands that dominate

A♥ Q♠ by a margin of 4 to 1 or more. It's a horrible hand to call a big raise with.

There's a time-honored saying, "Never go broke with a queen in you hand," and it's good advice to follow. It means you shouldn't voluntarily go all-in with A♥ Q♠ if you can help it. That's because of the very real possibility of getting an ace on the board and losing to an A-K hand (or to pocket aces, kings, or better).

Doyle Brunson says he hates playing A-Q because it's such a trap hand. In the 2007 WSOP $10,000 championship hold'em event, Doyle busted out early in the event holding… A♠ Q♥! The guy who busted him out was holding pocket queens and he flopped a set. So it looks like the advice about never going broke with a queen in your hand was destined to hold true for one of them.

World champ Phil Hellmuth also busted out early in the 2007 main event while holding A-Q. He also busted out early in the 2005 and 2006 main event while holding A-Q. That's three consecutive years. 2006 World champion Jamie Gold busted out early in the 2007 main event while holding Q♠ 9♠.

ANALOGY

Is there some way that I can figure out if my results (wins and losses) are the results of my playing ability and not just the results of random luck?

Yes, and that is to have a very large statistical sample from which to draw conclusions. The common sense approach is to understand that the longer you've been playing poker, and therefore the more hands you've played, the more certain it is that the results you're experiencing are the true results of your play. If you attempt a 4 to 1 draw with only 3 to 1 pot odds, the negative effects may not show up immediately. However, if you repeatedly try this 100 times, the long-term mathematical disadvantage will kick in and you'll be a big loser. If you've played forty hours of poker and are in the red, you might be a bad player. If you've played 2,000 hours of poker and you're in the red, you *are* a bad player.

There's an analogy that I like to explain to my students which they like and seem to understand. Picture yourself shooting a rifle at a target fifty yards away. You line up the target in the sights (or put the scope crosshairs right on it), you take a breath, slowly let some air out, and while timing it perfectly between heartbeats, you squeeze the trigger so that the gun goes off before you can react to it. The bullet flies down the rifle barrel at 3,000 feet per second and one-sixtieth of a second later, it rips through the target—exactly three inches off center to the right.

What happened? The bullet went exactly where you aimed it, even though you'd swear you had the gun aimed precisely at the bull's eye. The bullet hole in the target is proof of what actually happened. If the same thing is happening to you at poker, that is, you swear you're doing the best you know how to do, yet you're a big loser, you have to realize that there's something going on that you don't know about. This is where you have to believe your results are a true indicator of your ability and work backwards from there. This means you have a leak in your game that you're not aware of and there's probably some aspect of the game that you could understand better.

BACKDOOR
I will often have a hand like A♠ 9♠ and the flop is K♦ 10♦ 5♠, giving me little besides a backdoor spade draw. How can I figure out if it's worth it to draw to the backdoor flush or not?

YOU

FLOP

There are several factors:

1. Are you drawing to the nut flush?

2. Will you win if you spike an ace on the turn or river?

3. Will one of your spades make someone else a full house?

4. Do you have the right odds?

The most important of these is the question of odds. The chances of getting two running spades is 10/45 x 9/44, or about 1 in 22 times. That's about 4.5 percent, which is exactly what a one-card out is worth to you. It adds about the same value to your hand in the way that having a flush draw is only slightly more valuable than an open-end straight draw (nine outs vs. eight outs).

BAD BEATS
What's the worst bad beat you've ever had?
I was in a wild, crazy and extremely loose hold'em game at the Bingo Palace (now Palace Station) in Las Vegas in 1989. I was dealt the 8♣ 5♥. It was raised, reraised and capped by time the action got to me. I was in the 10-seat, right next to the dealer. One person had folded and it was going to be eight-handed if I mucked. I couldn't decide between folding because of the bad cards or calling to see the flop because of the action. I think I was distracted for a second because for some reason when it was my turn to act, I said, "Call," while folding my cards.

I meant to say "fold." One of the other players complained, saying that a verbal declaration made in turn is binding. He was right. I called the $14 bet and the dealer pushed my cards back to me. I put a chip on them and waited for the flop.

The flop was 7♦ 6♠ 4♥! I had flopped the nuts and the pot was already $112! The same players bet and raised and the betting was capped again. We lost one player and the pot was now about $200. The turn card was the 2♣ and the betting was capped again. The pot is now about $400 — in a $4/$8 game! I have the mortal nuts with no flush possible on the river. But I knew that a 5 or 8 on the river could lose the pot for me. I also didn't want the board to pair and lose to a full house.

The river card was the K♦ and now I had the nuts. The only thing that could ruin this hand was to have to split it, which was starting to look likely given all this action up to this point. We made it a $500 pot on the river — the biggest pot I have ever seen for this limit. There were three of us left. The first player turned over 7♣ 7♠ for a set. The second player showed 5♥ 3♥ for a smaller straight. And with unbelievable satisfaction and the biggest smile you've ever seen on a poker player's face, I turned over…J♦ 3♠ for — nothing!

Not a pair, not a straight. Nothing. The dealer had pushed back the wrong cards to me at the beginning of the hand and I had never looked at them.

My second-worst bad beat was when I had pocket aces and the flop was A-K-K. The jackpot was $10,000, and this was back in 1988 when the jackpots were split 80-20 with only the two players involved sharing it. My sole opponent was holding pocket kings, so we had flopped a jackpot. I was getting $8,000 and he was getting $2,000. Until the 6♣ came on the turn and the A♠ came on the river. I won the hand instead of losing it and that one card cost me $6,000.

BANKROLL
What size bankroll should I take to the game?
I like two answers. The first is don't take more money than you're comfortable losing in that game. The second is to figure out how much it might cost to play an average hand to the river and then decide how many of those average hands you are willing to lose before winning a hand and leaving the game. If it cost $20 to play a losing hand and you think you might have to play ten of these hands in order to have a better chance of surviving a while, then you'll need a bankroll of $200.

BLIND SITUATION OF A DIFFERENT SORT
I was recently in a game where a nearly-blind elderly player was seated in the 10-seat and the dealer read to him every card that came on the flop, turn and river every time he played a hand. This doesn't seem right even though I can't figure out exactly why. What do you think?
It's very wrong, even though it at first appears to be a cold-hearted thing to say. It gives him more time to

think about his hand than everyone else gets, and it's really wrong when the dealer reads the board to him and then adds, "No straight or flush is possible." If you can't see the cards, you can't play poker. You have to draw the line somewhere. And besides, who knows exactly how "blind" this player is, anyway?

BLUFFING
I recently won a huge pot by bluffing on the river and making the other player fold his hand. How can I get better at it and do it more often?
There are several things you should understand about bluffing. The first is the fact that most of the time that you successfully win a pot by bluffing, you really weren't bluffing at all! How can that be? It's because, given the nature of the community card aspect of the game, your opponent will often end up with a busted straight or flush draw on the river—just like you. Since neither of you has a hand you can call a bet with, whoever bets first wins the pot.

With experience, you will be able to recognize other favorable bluffing opportunities, usually when a possible straight or flush draw fails to materialize by the river or when you suspect weakness. In time, you'll come to develop a sense of awareness and timing that will tell you when to pick your best spots for bluffing.

But there's one other thing that I have discovered you can do to help with this part of the game. As you know, I'm a frequent note-taker. As an exercise to help my

198

game, I began to take notes every time I won a pot by bluffing. Of course, I waited a few minutes after the hand was over so as to not give away what I was recording. I took note of the positions of the players, the flop, turn and river, and who bet. After a while, and after collecting about twenty-five notes on successful bluffs, I began to see a pattern. I became more attuned to possible bluffing opportunities and I started to bluff more often. It worked.

Do you know what type of hand wins more hold'em pots than any other? It's an uncalled bet on the river. Put that fact to work for you — in the right spots.

Every time I try to bluff and get caught, I immediately muck my hand so no one can see what I was bluffing with. Now it's gotten to the point where I can't seem to win a single pot by bluffing. Any advice?
Picture this: You bet on the river and I call you. If you have a hand and were betting for value, you'd show your cards and probably win the pot. Or, at least you'd have a chance to win the pot. If I call and it turns out you were bluffing, all I have to do is sit there for a second while you realize that your bluff has been called and wait for you to muck your hand. The point is, it doesn't matter what I called you down with because you're never going to see my cards when you're bluffing. I'll call you every time with anything, everything and nothing because I'll be winning a lot of pots for the cost of only one bet.

Do you have a most memorable bluff story?
Of course. One time I was playing $10/$20 Omaha high/low split with an 8 or better for low qualifier. I was dealt A-2-3-K double suited. The betting was capped before the flop with eight-way action. I flopped the nut low draw, the nut flush draw and the Broadway draw. The betting was capped again and we lost a couple of players. The turn card gave me the other flush draw and we capped the betting again. The pot is now about $800. The river card was a blank for me—no low, no flush, no straight, no pair. I was first and bet it right out for $20. This was when I was young and still learning. I wouldn't do that today. Well, anyway, it went fold, fold, call. When he called I sheepishly said, "All I have is ace-high." He said, "Ace *what?* I couldn't believe what I heard. We had nearly the same type hand but I won with the A-K.

Another time I was holding 10♥ 9♥ and the board was 8♣ 7♦ 4♠ 2♥ 2♠. I had missed my straight draw. My sole opponent bet into me on the river and at the same time accidentally exposed his cards so that I could see he was holding K♣ 5♥. Knowing he had nothing but king-high, I raised him with my 10-high. He reraised. Hey, I didn't say my bluff worked.

What is a three-barrel bluff?
That's when a player bluffs on the flop, gets called, and then bluffs again on the turn. And when he gets called on the turn, he bluffs again on the river. Three bluffs—three barrels.

BOTTOM TWO PAIR

Why is it so hard to win with bottom two pair? You'd think that two pair is two pair regardless.

If you have 6-5 and the flop is K-6-5, your hand is not nearly as good as it looks. That's because there are so many cards that can come on the turn and river to beat you. Another king usually makes trips for someone. A player holding a king can hit his kicker to make a higher two pair, a pair can come on the turn and river, and bottom two pair often means there's a straight draw out there against you.

In this example, an ace might make someone aces-up, a king makes trips, a queen, jack or 10 usually makes someone kings-up, and a 9 makes a straight for the lucky player holding 8-7. Play cautiously when you flop bottom two pair and be aware that the more players there are in the hand, the more vulnerable it is. Try not to send good money after bad when it looks like you can't win with the hand. And most of all, remember that a low two pair only improves to a low full house.

CALLING STATION

I play in a game where there's almost always one or more players who call every bet, every time, all the way to the river. How do I play against these players and how do I take advantage of this?

These players are called *calling stations,* and if there's one thing for sure, you're never going to run them off a hand. One of my favorite quotes about limit poker is: "It takes a long time to beat bad players." That's because the way they play effectively takes away one of your weapons—the bluff. If you bet into one of these players, you need to have a hand when you're called. So, the first advice is to remember that ahead of time. When you call before the flop and the calling station calls right after you, say to yourself, "Okay, I'm probably going to need a hand at the river and I won't be able to bluff."

You can start to bet weaker hands for value on the river since you know you'll usually be called with almost nothing. You can save money by not bluffing as often. Be patient and the money will come, although it will be very slow in coming.

CARD COVER
What is a card cover?
Just as each player is charged with the responsibility of playing only his hand, each player is also responsible for protecting his cards while the hand is in play. This is so that they can't be accidentally mixed with other cards. You do this by placing a weighty object, called a *card cover* (or *card protector*) on them.

Most players use poker chips for the job. You might have seen Johnny Chan and his orange or Humberto Brenes with his toy shark, or other players with various other things. For years I used a small railroad pocket watch. Everyone who saw it instantly admired the watch and the idea and one fellow player admired it so much that it was stolen from me when I was away from the table.

I now use an 1820 large cent. The U.S. Mint made 4,407,550 of them that year and you can get a very nice one from a coin shop for about $20 to $40, depending on the condition. It's about the size of the modern day Kennedy fifty-cent piece and it's a beautiful work of art.

CARD TRICK

I noticed you taught a card trick in your *Big Book of Poker*. What was the reason for that?

It was an exercise in developing skill at card memory, concentration and confidence—all skills necessary to be a good poker player. There's also a slight intimidating effect. Anyone who can count down a deck of cards will certainly earn respect at the poker table.

CASINO POKER ROOM COMPS

I know poker players don't get comped like the big blackjack, craps, roulette and baccarat losers in the main casino, but how can I find out exactly what I can ask for in my poker room and what I can get?

You can find out exactly what every Las Vegas poker room offers for comps at www.allvegaspoker.com.

"CHECK DARK"

What does *check dark* really mean and why would someone do that? Isn't he taking away his own options before he even sees the flop or the next card?

The player who's first to act will often have a hand that's weak, yet might still be worth a crying call under the circumstances. This player will usually call with that weak hand after you bet. The only option that he's taking away from himself is that of betting. He can still check, check-raise, fold or raise. Since he doesn't want to bet, it might mean that he's trying to get you to bluff or bet a weak hand yourself. Alternatively, he might be trying to put doubts in your mind about his hand and he might want you to also check. Also, the player who just checked dark might be waiting for an all-or-nothing card to make a straight for a flush on the next round. You just have to know the players you're up against.

COLLUSION
I've heard that open collusion between two or more players is actually tolerated and it's not cheating. Is this right? How can that be true?
You've almost got it right—in a way. Cheating is strictly forbidden at all times under all circumstances, but there is a form of collusion that is actually an accepted part of poker strategy and is a part of the game.

It applies only during a tournament when someone is all-in and there are two or more players with chips still contesting the pot. This is where the collusion part comes in. Knowledgeable tournament players know in advance, before they even come to the tournament, that their strategy will be to check the hand down against other players who are all in. This means that there will be no time when there will be a bet and a player with chips will have to fold. This allows every player with chips to stay in the hand to the river, thus affording everyone the best possible chance to beat the all-in player. If they beat the all-in player, someone will win a small pot, but more importantly, they will all move up the tournament payout ladder — and that's what all the checking was about.

The only time anyone should bet is when they make the nuts or are otherwise certain they're going to win the hand and knock out the all-in player. This isn't true collusion in the strict negative sense of the word, it's just that the word comes the closest to describing the situation.

You should realize that you can also apply this to live games as well. If the all-in player is, for whatever reason, an undesirable in your game, you can all collude to bust him out. I try to do this when I can get a short-stacked player busted out so he can be replaced by a new player with a full buy-in. It gets more money on the table.

My wife and I love to play poker in our local casino poker room. Yet, every time we introduce ourselves to others as married to each other, we get the obvious nonverbal message that we are in collusion with each other and we're going to cheat everyone else at the table. This is not true! How do we handle this situation?
You have nothing to hide and you have nothing to be ashamed of. Be sure to always make sure that everyone knows that you're married to each other. Be proud of it. I've played in games against married couples where they did not even acknowledge each other at the table and no one knew that they were together until they left the game

and proceeded hand-in-hand to the cashier's cage. I think it's that type of couple you have to worry about.

Do not softplay each other. Bet and raise your spouse as you would any other player. Don't forget that check-raising is also a part of the game. Don't give each other "looks" while waiting for one of you to act against the other. Don't root out loud for your spouse. Don't talk when one of you is in a hand. Try not to sit next to each other. Other players will worry about nonverbal communication under the table.

And one more bit of advice that I have learned at the table just by observing: Ladies, if it's just you and your husband in the hand at the end, and he bets into you, you should almost always call with anything that can catch a bluff. No matter how much you think your husband loves you and wouldn't take advantage of you, he *will* try to bluff you out every time on the river, while acting like he has a monster hand. Guaranteed.

COMFORT
When I play poker, I like to have my cell phone, wallet, medicine, notepad, organizer, pens, reading glasses, emergency reading material and whatever with me. But I don't want to carry a backpack or a briefcase. What can I do?
You asked the right guy! Ever been to a hunting goods store or a sports outfitter? You can buy shirts, vests, jackets and coats with more pockets on them than you

have stuff. They fit well, they're comfortable, and they even provide some warmth.

DEALS

Whenever I make the final table in a tournament, there's always talk of making a deal. How do I decide what to do?

There's a mathematical formula that takes into account the number of players remaining, their stack sizes and the amount each place is paid. The formula is complicated and difficult to apply with ease when you actually need it during a tournament. However, there's a few simple guidelines you can follow that will help you figure out whether to play on or take the money and run.

1. The chances of placing in the money are directly proportional to the amount of chips you hold in relation to the other players. In other words, the player with the most chips will probably place in the money and the player with the shortest stack probably won't. If you have the most chips, you should usually prefer to not deal, and if you have the shortest stack, you should be begging for a deal.

2. Look around the table and try to determine everyone's level of experience and tournament skill. If you think you can beat them—don't take the deal. If they're clearly superior players, take the deal.

3. Take a look at the payouts for first, second and third places. Compare the deal amount to these payouts. Very often you'd have to win the tournament outright to get more than what you're being offered in the deal. Compare your estimate of making one of the top three places to the deal amount. I usually take the deal if the deal amount is more than what third place pays. You'd have to win second place to get more than that. I'll take that deal because things get more uncertain as the blinds rise and play becomes more of a crapshoot.

DUPLICATION

I've noticed that when I read the odds for drawing to a hand on the turn and river, that they're not exactly a 2 to 1 ratio of each other. In other words, if my percentage of making a hand on the turn is 36 percent, then it seems that the percentage chance of making the hand on the river should be exactly half that, or 18 percent. But it's not and all of the numbers for the river are a little bit off like that. Why is that?

It's due to a mathematical phenomenon called *duplication*. Incidentally, I get a lot of email from readers who tell me my tables are wrong, and it's because they don't understand duplication. It works like this: Assume you have Q♥ J♥ and the flop is 10♣ 9♠ 2♦.

YOU

BOARD

You need a king or 8 to make your straight. You will make the hand 31.5 percent of the time by the river but if you miss on the turn you will make the hand 17.4 percent of the time. Half of 31.5 percent is 15.75 percent, not 17.4 percent. So, why is that?

It's because of what happens when you do make your hand. This is what the turn and river cards could be:

K-K

K-9

9-K

9-9

Sometimes you make your hand twice and the duplicate card accounts for the mathematical difference.

The same thing happens with a four-flush draw on the flop. If you have four hearts you only need one more, but sometimes (4.545 percent of the time) you'll get two hearts.

EXPOSED CARDS
I accidentally exposed one of my cards before the flop and before the action got to me. What's the rule on this?
If you did it yourself through no fault of the dealer, you have to keep and play that card until you voluntarily fold the hand. The two blinds and the player on the button are supposed to get their original first card. If one of those cards flashes, then it's a mandatory redeal. If one of their second cards flash, it's not a redeal and that card is replaced according to the poker room procedures.

My card quickly flashed while it was in the air on the way to me. It landed face down and I don't think anyone saw it. Can I keep it?
Any card that has turned face up, flashed, probably flashed, or could have possibly flashed is presumed to have fully flashed and is automatically a dead card. This is to prevent having to settle any question of to what degree it did flash, who did and didn't see it, and to remove any possibility of an unfair advantage over the incident.

FINDING A CASINO POKER ROOM
I don't live in Las Vegas but I would like to go to a public brick and mortar poker room. How can I find one near me?
There's an awesome new website called www.Pokermashup.com that will locate the ten nearest poker rooms to your home. Just enter your zip code and it will show you a map with the distance and directions to each poker room.

FLUSH
I've heard it said that a king-high flush draw is almost as good as the ace-high flush draw. Is this true?
The first thing that's definitely true is that no king-high flush draw can make the nuts like the ace-high flush draw. Even so, the king-high flush is still a strong hand because the ace of your suit will often not be in play and, even if it is, it will not be suited three-fourths of the time.

If you hold K♥ 9♥ against nine other players, then the A♥ is one of fifty other cards. Eighteen of those cards are in the hands of the other players and thirty-two are still in the deck. So, it is 18 to 32, or 9 to 16 in favor of the A♥ not being out against you. If it is in someone's hand, then it's 3 to 1 against it being paired with another heart. Three hearts on the board will make you a flush, but will make only a four-flush for the other player. Only four hearts on the board can kill your flush, presuming that the A♥ is in an opponent's hand. You also have the wonderful possibility of having it come on the board or of it being dealt to one of your opponents who mucks it before the flop because of a bad kicker.

I like king-high flush draws. They usually win when you make them. I'll play them like the nut flush draw until I get indications that I should back off.

FOLDING BIG HANDS
I heard that Phil Hellmuth actually folded an open-end straight flush draw during a big tournament. Can this possibly be true?
Yes. Phil flopped a 9♦ 10♦ J♦ Q♦ draw with two cards to come. He had 15 outs twice which gave him over a 50% percent chance of making a straight or a flush, which would have won the hand. However, being the world champion that he is, he didn't see the situation as most hold'em players would. He was not impressed by the fact that we're talking about a high poker hand like a straight flush. He saw it for what it really was—essentially a coin flip. He was playing to win the tournament and didn't want to risk being busted out half-way through with a strong chance of not surviving the hand.

FREE CARD ON THE FLOP
I've heard that you're not supposed to give a free card on the flop. You're always supposed to bet on the flop. Can you explain what this is all about?
You almost got it right. The actual rule of thumb is that you shouldn't give a free card when there's an ace and no pair on the flop if you have anything at all worth protecting. That's because the next card (the turn) will

always be able to complete a possible straight draw if your opponents are holding the right cards. These draws will most often be gutshot draws so it would usually be correct for them to fold to a bet on the flop.

GHOST HAND

What is a ghost hand and is it something that figures into my poker strategy?

A ghost hand is one that is made up of all or most of the same cards you saw in the hand played right before it. For example, I saw a hand played where one player made four fives and the other player made three kings. The dealer awarded the pot and proceeded to shuffle and deal the next hand. The kings and fives were bunched together and the shuffle was sloppy and not up to standard. I was dealt the K♣ 5♠ and I called solely because I knew these cards were close together in the deck. Sure enough, two kings and a 5 hit the board and I won with a full house, a hand that I never would have played except for the fact that I was looking for—and found—a ghost hand.

The answer to the second part of the question is yes. You should pay attention and recognize the possibility of an upcoming ghost hand.

HEADS-UP

When heads-up, how do the blinds work and who bets first?

There are always two blinds, the small blind is on the button and he acts first.

HISTORY
When was the first public poker room opened?
Entrepreneur John Davis opened the first public poker room in the Crescent House Casino in New Orleans in 1827!

HORSE
What is HORSE and how can it possibly be related to poker?
HORSE is an acronym for five poker games:

> **H**old'em
> **O**maha
> **R**azz
> **S**tud (7-card)
> **E**ight or better 7-card stud

Each game is played for either one round or for a certain length of time and then the next game in the rotation is played. It's a test of a player's overall poker ability. Good HORSE players are recognized as the best in the world by the top professionals. In 2006, it was introduced as a WSOP event with a $50,000 buy-in. The first winner was David "Chip" Reese.

HOYLE, EDMOND
Who is Hoyle and what does "According to Hoyle" mean?
Edmond Hoyle (1679-1769) was an English barrister (lawyer) and serious card player. He wrote a book in 1742 called, *A Short Treatise on the Game of Whist*, which was the first written rules for card games. His book was used as the authoritative source to settle card

game disputes and soon everyone played by the rules as laid out according to Hoyle. In short order the term *According to Hoyle* came to mean *by the book*, and was used to describe most all games.

American-style poker did not exist in 1742 although there was an English game called Brag that eventually evolved into poker a century later. Hoyle never played poker, never knew what it was, and died a century before poker gained nationwide popularity in the United States.

IMAGE
What should my image be at the table? I never know what to do or how to do it.
I believe that concern over an image is greatly overrated. If you're a solid, winning low-limit player, your image should take care of itself. Just remember to be polite, personable and friendly if you can.

However, if you still want to deliberately project a certain image, you should let your cards do it for you in the beginning of your playing session. If you get a run of bad, unplayable cards, you will appear to be a tight player to your opponents. Continue to play tight until you determine that it's profitable to change gears and loosen up.

If you get a run of great, playable hands when you first sit down, and you're winning every other hand, then continue to play as loose as you can without giving up your advantage. Then, when you're ready, tighten up. When you do play a hand, you'll be paid off very well.

JACKPOTS
What is the weirdest hold'em jackpot you've ever seen?
One player held 2♠ 2♦ and another player held 5♥ 3♥. The final board was 2♣ 2♥ 3♠ 3♦ 3♣. Four deuces lost to four treys. The really weird part is that this jackpot met the poker room requirement that both players' hole cards must play and the kicker must beat the board. This is an illegal requirement that gets overturned by the State Gaming Commission whenever it's formally challenged. The rule requires you to play six or even seven cards as your poker hand in order to settle a side bet (the jackpot).

What happens if a jackpot is hit at my table but the management won't award it because the winner's kicker doesn't beat the board?
I'll tell you what should happen: Every state has a gaming commission rule that says "All disputes will be settled by the State Gaming Commission." Someone in the hand should tell the poker room manager, "I'm making this a dispute." This takes the question out of his hands and gives it to the Gaming Commission. The player should then document everything and take everyone's identification as if he were going to pay the jackpot. Make sure surveillance does their part just as if it were a valid jackpot. One of the players will have to make a formal complaint at the Gaming Commission

office. Upon review, the gaming commission will over-rule the poker room management and award the jack-pot. This may take a few days or weeks. This is what has happened in every jurisdiction where the rule has been challenged. You cannot change the rules of poker to settle a side bet.

Why can't you discuss the possibility of a jackpot while the hand is in progress?

That's what the poker room management tells you but it's also an illegal requirement. As long as no one is cheating, there is no collusion, and no one is violat-ing the one-player-per-hand rule, the players can and may talk about the cards on the board. Management doesn't like you doing this because it slightly increases the chance that a jackpot will be hit when more players are aware of the possibility.

What is a jackpot chaser?

It's a player who has a choice of more than one poker room to play in and he lets the size of the jackpot and the requirements to hit it be the sole determining fac-tors in where he plays. It's a player who is almost always sitting in the hold'em game with the biggest jackpot. Don't forget that an Omaha jackpot is about four times easier to hit than a hold'em jackpot. Just multiply the size of the Omaha jackpot by four and then compare that number with the size of the hold'em jackpot. If you're a jackpot chaser, then that comparison will tell you which game to play in.

LIMIT
Which limit do you think is better: $4/$8 or $1-$4-$8-$8?

The only difference between these two games is that in one you must bet either $4 or $8 and in the other you may bet any amount between $1-$4 and then $1-$8. The more options your opponents have, the more opportunities they have to make mistakes. The game that offers them a choice of how much to bet also gives them a chance to make the wrong choice. The $1-$4-$8-$8 is much better for you because your opponents will often bet $1, $2, or $3 when they should be betting $4, and they will bet $1 to $7 when they should be betting $8. In doing so, they invite you to correctly try to draw out on them. Every dollar less than the maximum bet is $1 you save.

Is $3/$6 or $1-$4-$8-$8 the better game?

If you understand the above advice, then you now know that the $1-$4-$8-$8 game is much better.

Why does the $5/$10 hold'em game seem to be so tough and hard to beat?

It's because it's the first limit above the white chip ($1) games. It's the lowest limit red chip ($5) game and players who have just moved up in limit are going to play very tight. They are usually solid players who are very careful at the new, higher limit.

What do you consider to be the best limit for a good, lower limit player?

This might surprise you, but I truly believe that the best game for good, lower limit players is $10/$20. My objective is to help you become a good enough player that you can be a winner at $10/$20. If you buy-in for a rack of chips, which is just about right, you will buy-in for $500. That's one-hundred red chips. It's the same as playing $2/$4 with a $100 buy-in. $10/$20 is the same as $2/$4—only you're playing with red chips instead of white chips. The players will be better, which makes them easier to read. They generally have what they're supposed to have, you won't have as many bad beats with weird cards, the game is much faster, and best of all, the rake is a significantly smaller part of the pot. The limit is high enough that you can now beat the rake.

Another good reason to play $10/$20 is that it is actually more protective of your bankroll than $1-$4-$8-$8 is. If you call a bet on every round, and lose the hand, you will lose only twelve chips in the big game, but you will lose twenty-two chips with that same hand in the lower limit game. If you can buy-in five times in the lower limit game, why don't you save up and buy in once in the red chip game? If you're a good player, I guarantee you'll like it.

LOOSE GAMES

How do I play in these wild, fast, crazy and very loose games that seem to take place every weekend? These games have very big swings.

There are several things you can do. Remember that it's the quality of your decisions that matter in the long run. Keep in mind the following things.

1. Don't draw to hands that aren't the nuts.

2. Raise and make them pay when you have the best hand (they'll call—that's what makes it a loose game).

3. Don't slowplay.

4. Bluff much less (you'll always get called).

5. Have a long-term view of the game.

6. Don't start to play too loose yourself.

7. It's okay to loosen up your starting hand requirements a little bit, but don't go too far.

LUCK

How can I tell if I'm a good player experiencing a run of bad luck or if I'm a bad player and don't realize it?

The short answer is that the longer you play the more certain it is that the results you're experiencing are actually due to your skill, or lack thereof. Good players can run bad for months. Bad players can run good for months. An accepted rule of thumb is that if you're losing more than 300 big bets in the game you usually play in, then there's about a 95 percent chance that it's due to lack of skill, and not bad luck.

MATH
The most mathematically improbable thing I've ever seen in a hold'em game was when three players each flopped a set on the flop. What are the odds against this happening?
78,165 to 1

MONEY MANAGEMENT
What is the Kelly System of money management?
In simple terms, it's the idea that for every time you gamble, you shouldn't risk more than a certain percentage of your total bankroll.

To quote myself from my earlier book, *The Big Book of Poker*, "No style, type or form of money management will work if you play a game of skill without the skill."

I seem to be unable to set aside $100 for another buy-in for the next time I want to play after I've had a winning session. I always end up spending the money that I'd rather save for a buy-in. Do you have any ideas?
Been there. Done that. I didn't like it, either. There are two things that I've done that worked well for me. The first is, when I cash out, I get a $100 black chip and then I put it in my pocket and walk out of the casino. Of course, I can't spend it at the mall or the burger

drive-through. It's with me when I go back to the poker room for my next buy-in. The other thing I do is to put my $100 bill into a slot machine and then immediately cash out a $100 ticket and then take that home with me. It's good for a minimum of ninety days and maybe more. It'll say on the ticket.

MONTANA BANANA
Why is nine-deuce (9-2) called Montana Banana?
Because it was proposition #29 on the ballot that legalized public poker when it was passed in Montana.

ODDS
Why is knowing poker odds so important? I thought poker was mostly about poker hands, betting, bluffing and knowing your opponents.
Limit poker is really just one long series of offers of proposition bets with a certain amount of money being either won or lost depending on whether you make a winning or losing bet. Over the course of a lifetime of poker playing, you make these same bets over and over with your cumulative running total of your wins or losses being the reflection of the quality of the bets (decisions) you've made.

Imagine we are going to flip a fair coin one million times. Every time it comes up heads, you pay me $1, and every time it comes up tails, I'll pay you 90¢. You can easily see that you're guaranteed to be about a $50,000 loser. That's because you weren't getting the right odds on your bet. That's what it's like to play poker. Every time it is your turn to make a decision, you're really trying to decide if you're getting the right odds on what you're about to do. To really oversimplify the explanation, if you're a loser at limit poker, it's because you're consistently making and calling bets when the pot is not big enough to justify it.

ODDS CALCULATOR
Is there a computer program that I can use to calculate hand odds for hold'em?
Yes. You can calculate hold'em and Omaha odds at www.cardplayer.com. They also have a hand-held odds calculator that you can order for just $4.99.

OUTS
The mathematical tables listing all the outs for the various draws are complicated and overwhelming. Is there a lazy man's shortcut or rule of thumb that I can use to simplify them?
Yes. It's the 4 x 2 rule. If you have nine outs on the turn, as in a four-flush draw, then multiply 9 x 4 to get 36. This tells you that you have roughly a 36 percent chance of making the draw. The true percentage is 35 percent. If you have nine outs on the river, multiply by two. This gives you a rough 16 percent when the true percentage is 17.4 percent. Close enough.

PARKING
How do you handle the limited parking or no parking spaces available when you go to a busy poker room?
This is going to surprise you, but I *always* get the exact parking space I want every time, no matter how busy

the place is. That's because I always deliberately park as far away from the poker room as I can — within reason. I use the time it takes to walk to the building to go over my strategy, make some advance decisions, get in the right frame of mind to play poker, and put my game face on.

After the game, I use the time it takes to walk back to the car to…well, if you don't know, then I'd like to refer you to the section on *Mistakes Made After the Game* elsewhere in this book.

PARLAY PLAYER
What is a parlay? What is a parlay player?
A parlay is the process of winning with your initial buy-in and then moving up in limit with your newly-won stake. A typical example of a parlay for a poker player would be to buy in with $200 in a $4/$8 hold'em game with the idea that if he won $300, he would then enter the $10/$20 hold'em game with his $500.

What are the best parlay stories you've ever heard of?
#1: When I was a beginning player in Las Vegas back in the 1980s, I would buy into a $2/$4 hold'em game with only $40 at the Mint (now part of Binion's), run that up to over $100 and then get into the $3/$6 game across the street at the Four Queens and run that up to several hundred dollars. I would then get in the $10/$20 hold'em game at either the Golden Nugget or Binions where I would win more than $1,000. The games were that good back then. What makes this a good parlay

story for me is the fact that I was able to do this regularly instead of just one time. I've often been asked why I would start over in the small game if I was able to win so much in the big game. Obviously, the answer is that I violated a cardinal rule of being a professional poker player: I spent my poker-playing bankroll.

#2: Here's the best parlay story of all. I know a poker player who put $100 into his new PokerStars account and by playing smart low-limit poker, he ran it up to over $6,000. "Big deal," you say, "What's go great about that?" He got the $100 deposit by making a deposit of his own at the sperm bank!

PATIENCE
I know there are many skills that I must master to be a winning poker player. Which skill or skills are most important that I could start working on right away?
The two most important skills to begin with are understanding the poker odds and having patience. Your job as a professional poker player is to make correct decisions. Most of the time that correct decision will be to fold. That's probably the best decision about 85 percent of the time, no matter what type of poker you're playing. It's boring. The first incorrect decision that the average player willingly and knowingly makes is to call that first bet when he should fold. Don't do that! It's your job to wait for the other players to begin to do that.

Being patient has several good advantages. It keeps you from playing losing hands and busting out of the game.

It keeps you in the game in case the jackpot gets hit. You will get a free ride in the big blind and win some hands that you'd never call with from another position. When you do play a hand, you'll occasionally flop the nuts. You have a good chance to win the first hand you play, which will take off some of the pressure and give your bankroll a slight cushion.

When you patiently wait for the right cards in the right position, you'll usually be up against players who are playing the wrong cards in the wrong positions. If you can repeat this situation many times in the course of the game, the chips will come.

PERCENTAGE CALL
What is a percentage call? Other players tell me that that's what they're doing when they call me on the river, but I don't get it.
It's just another way of saying that the player is calling because the pot is very big and he can beat a bluff or he's calling with a hand that has a very small chance to win against a legitimate hand, but he's getting big pot odds. He's acknowledging that he probably has a loser, but he does expect to win the hand in this situation every once in a while, making it a long-run profitable call.

Whenever I make a percentage call and lose the pot, I often tell the bettor, "I had the right odds to be wrong."

PET PEEVES
Do you have any poker related pet peeves?
You bet I do. The first is clueless, totally oblivious cocktail waitresses who try to force-deliver my drink order when I'm in the middle of playing a hand. The second is dealers who instantly tell me it's my turn to act before I've even had a chance to look at the second card he's dealt me. The third is poker room managers who assume that every player wants to play at a full ten-handed table. And the last is poker room managers who've been in the business so long that they've forgotten what a customer is.

PLAYING BAD
What are the hidden costs of playing bad?
You lose more than just your buy-in. That money has to be replaced by the next poker bankroll you get and starts a chain reaction that ultimately affects your bankroll for the whole year. Busting out keeps you from being in the game when your seat gets hot. Though it's nothing you can count on (but it does happen), not having a bankroll also keeps you from being at the table when the jackpot is hit.

POKER TABLES
How many poker tables are there in all the public poker rooms and casinos in the world?
As of early 2008, there were over 6,800 legal poker tables in operation.

POKER VERSUS BLACKJACK

What's the big advantage of poker over that other casino game of skill—blackjack?

Professional blackjack players who are able to count cards and adjust their bets accordingly can sometimes, but not often, be in a situation where they might have as much as a 5 percent edge over the house for a few consecutive bets. Players who demonstrate skill at blackjack are carefully watched by surveillance and security and are subject to being evicted from the property, being read the trespass law, having their chips and money confiscated by the casinos, and threatened with imprisonment if they try to return.

When was the last time you had a 60 percent advantage over another player (your A-K versus his A-J) and you got threatened with all that when you won the hand? The fact that a casino considers a 5 percent disadvantage on a few hands at blackjack to be a threat to their existence ought to convince you what a great game poker is for you with a 60 percent advantage.

POSITION

I've read all the books telling me why I need to have good cards in early position, but I still don't get it. Can you help?

Obviously, a poker analogy won't help, so let's try this: Are you familiar with the game show *The Price is Right* with Bob Barker (and now with Drew Carey)? Three contestants spin a wheel with the one getting the highest score going to the final showcase. They each get two spins of the wheel to add to their total. The first contestant might spin a 30 (with 100 being the best score).

But common sense says that he can't hold at 30 because it's so easy for one of the other two to top that score. He has to spin again to achieve a total that can't be beat by two players who each have two spins. The second contestant doesn't need to score in the 80s or 90s because there's only one player behind him, and he might go over 100 and be disqualified. The first contestant needs a high score, the second contestant only needs a good score, and the last contestant can win with anything.

That's the way it is in poker. The earlier you have to act, the better your hand has to be in order to match up to all of those players who have all of those good cards behind you. You don't know exactly what you have to beat so you have to insure yourself by making sure you hold good cards.

PREFLOP RAISING
When a player raises before the flop, how can I be sure he has pocket aces?
You can never be sure. However, there are a few indicators that might lead you to this possibility. If he watches each player intently as they act on his raise, it's because he's watching them put money in a pot he expects to win. That might mean he knows he has the best hand at this point. If he actually says he's disappointed when everyone calls, but no one reraises, he probably has

pocket aces. If you reraise and he puts in the last raise, he quite possibly has A-A or perhaps K-K.

What would you say is the #1 overall best reason for raising before the flop?
To make your decisions *after* the flop that much easier. It also does the following:

- It helps you read other players' hands.

- You get value for your hand

- You make second-best hands pay you off.

- You set up a continuation bet on the flop.

- You put yourself in a position to bluff.

What's the problem with raising with hands like A♠ 4♦, K♥ 9♣ and Q♥ 8♠?
Unless you're raising to steal the blinds, the problem is that anyone who calls you should have you already beat. For example, if you raise with A-4, another player with an ace will only call you if his kicker is very good. By raising, you're playing the hand for a double bet and you might feel compelled to follow it up with a continuation bet on the flop. Now you get to lose a lot of money.

RABBIT HUNTING
What is rabbit hunting? I know poker has some interesting words and phrases, but I can't figure this one out.
When the hand is over before all the cards are dealt and someone wants to know what the next card would have

been, he's *rabbit hunting*. You don't have to ever do it yourself. It's a sign that you're becoming a better player when you can let a hand go without rabbit hunting. All you need to do is familiarize yourself with the general odds on draws and that will tell you all you need to know.

RACE

What is a *race* as it applies to poker?
When one player gets all of their money in the pot before the flop and gets called by another player, and there's nothing left to do but deal the flop, turn and river—it's a race. This most often occurs during a no-limit tournament.

RAISE

How do I handle it when I raise before the flop and get absolutely no help from the flop?
Usually, you will want to give the impression that you have the winning hand, and that means you should follow up with a continuation bet. But be sensible. If you have A♠ K♠ and you're facing three players with a flop of 9♣ 8♦ 7♥, you're probably not going to win this hand. Realistically evaluate your chances of winning the hand, either by bluffing or by having the best hand at the end. If you do decide to bet, act like you have five aces. Confidence is a pot winner.

Is there a best time to raise?
It depends on what your goal is. If you're raising for value, the best time to raise is when you know they'll

call and you won't lose. For me, that's on the turn. If you're raising to make players fold, then before the flop is the best time to raise. If you're raising to gain information, I suggest you reevaluate your motive and ask yourself if the info you gain is worth the cost. I've put some thought and done a little research into the question, and I've decided that raising to gain information is usually not worth it.

What's the best bit of advice you can give me about raising? I like raising for all the obvious reasons, but I'd like to be really smart about it.
If you recall all those games in the past where you had huge wins, you might realize that you were in a game where another player was raising and reraising for all the wrong reasons at the same time you were raising and reraising for all the right reasons. Simple, huh? It's just another way of describing a very loose game, only now you know why you were a winner.

RAKE
Why is the exact amount of the rake so important? Why should I care if it's $5 or $4?
Playing in a ten-handed raked game is the same as playing in an eleven-handed game where one certain player wins a guaranteed $5 per hand. At thirty-five hands per hour, that's $175 that disappears from the table every hour. And here's the part that most players don't think about: You can *never* win that money back, as you could from a real player. In an eight-hour playing session, this "player" will win as much as $1,400. Who wins that

much in a low limit beginner's hold'em game? The poker room does, that's who. And that's $1,400 for each table that's in action.

Get this: If ten players each start a game with a $100 buy-in, and they are not replaced by new players when they bust out, *everyone* in the game will go broke in five hours and forty minutes. The rake will take all of the money in less than six hours.

RANDOM
How do I randomize my decisions?
This is a pretty broad question. No matter what the decision is or at what stage of the game it comes, the point is to make a decision based on a factor totally unrelated to the play of the hand or the cards in play. The question assumes that the decision will be between two or more equally good choices—and this is a prerequisite!—so you want to hide the fact that the decision was made randomly.

One of the most common tips I hear about is to look at the second hand on your watch. If it just passed an odd number, you decide one way and you go the other way if it just passed an even number. Some players go by the day on the calendar. They decide to play a certain way all day on odd-numbered days and the other way on even-numbered days.

Some players make their decisions based solely on who the dealer is. I know one player who will only raise before the flop with pocket aces, kings and queens and with other pocket pairs only when they are both red cards (diamonds and hearts).

I think the best solution is for you to actively try to answer this question for yourself. Make your decisions based on some personal factor and then keep it a secret.

RECORDS

I recognize the necessity, value and benefits of keeping records of my poker playing, but I am very, very lazy about it? Any suggestions?

There are dozens of details you can keep records of, but I think it would work for you if you just kept the minimum facts in a blank bank check register devoted exclusively to this purpose. That would be date, where you played, the limit, the game and your net win or loss.

RIVER

I always get confused over whether I should bet or check with an average-strength hand on the river. Is there some guideline or rule of thumb?

There's an involved, complicated mathematical formula that you can use to compute your best course of action down to the nth degree, but that's no fun. You won't be giving up very much if you just answer this simple question for yourself: "How much am I going to like it if I bet and get called?" That ought to help you decide what to do.

RIVERBOAT POKER ROOMS

Are the riverboat poker rooms in the central United States any different from the poker rooms in Nevada, California and Atlantic City? What's your opinion of them?

The biggest difference is the fact that they have what's called a "loss limit" law. That means that you're allowed to lose only $500 per two-hour period. They enforce this law by using the player's club card to control and monitor buy-ins. You need one of these cards just to get inside the door. This law has the effect of keeping the stakes of the poker games relatively low so that it's difficult to lose $500 in two hours. This means that there aren't any high-limit and large blind no-limit games.

There's another difference that's even more important from the poker player's perspective. It's what I'm going to call the "homogenous factor." Most of the riverboat cities with poker rooms are not big tourist destinations like Las Vegas. They are a relatively closed society from a poker room clientele point of view. This means that all of the regular poker players consistently play against each other in the long run.

It's like being in a small town where everyone knows each other very well, even though the actual population of the city might be a half-million or more. The dealer knows every player by name and the game he usually likes to play. The players have hundreds, if not thousands of hours at the table playing against each other. They know each other's strengths and weaknesses and they've adapted to each other's style of play. And the really interesting part is that most of the adapting to each other that they've done has been a result of unconscious modifications rather than a deliberate attempt to improve their game.

As a result, so many of them play so much alike that it's totally killed the action. Almost no one ever raises before the flop unless he's holding aces or kings. And when there is a raise, almost no one ever calls and there is certainly hardly ever a reraise. Most of the time the action goes bet-call or check-bet-call. Many times there's no call on the flop. There's almost never a raise on the river by the player who has the nuts because the other players don't bet on the river without the nuts.

In the past few months I've played about fifty hours of poker in the St. Louis Ameristar poker room. I don't ever recall seeing the betting capped (a bet and three raises) in any game at any time. A player who was raised on the river usually just called. Whenever one player had the nuts and the other had the second nuts, they established that fact with one bet and raise and then the action was over. That's tight! Between the high rake and the no-action-unless-you're-beat style of play, you cannot beat these type of games.

ROCK

How do I take advantage of, and make a profit from, very tight players, also known as rocks?

Think about what makes them a rock. They don't play that many hands, they don't take chances, and they don't put money in the pot unless they have an almost guaranteed lock. This makes them very easy to read. The weakness of a rock is that he folds too much. The secret is for you to still be in the hand after he folds. How you accomplish this is up to your poker intelligence. Be sensible and try to recognize those flops where it seems a rock won't call. In that case, you can try betting because you know he'll fold and not necessarily because you have a good hand.

SEATING

The players on my immediate left just left the game. Should I take his seat?

I think you should, unless you have a very good reason to want to stay where you are. It's a fact that in a hold'em game money tends to move around the table in a clockwise manner. You should have that new money on your right so that that player will always have to act on his hand before you do. If he sits down on your left, you'd have to start check-raising him to get the same effect as if he were on your right.

SECOND PAIR

I know that it's not possible for someone to have flopped top pair every time, and I know that I will often have the best hand when I've flopped second

pair with a good kicker. Yet, when I bet second pair, it seems that I'm usually wrong about my judgment. Can you help?

Since it's obvious that everyone plays mostly high cards, you can see that you're not likely to have the best hand when the flop is A-Q-7 and you hold a queen. That's because it's so likely that someone else will have an ace in his hand. If you have A♣ 8♣ and the flop is 9-8-3, you have a better chance of having the best hand because players are less likely to play a 9 than an ace. Use discretion and you'll start to see better results.

You also increase your chances of success if there's no possible four-flush draw or reasonable straight draw.

SHORT-HANDED

I know that you're supposed to play a lot looser in a short-handed game, but I'm having a hard time forcing myself to play what I ordinarily consider to be weak or bad hands. How can I learn to play short-handed?

The first obvious answer is to play in a lot of short-handed games and then slowly loosen up your starting hand requirements. Start raising and calling raises with slightly progressively weaker hands until you find an equilibrium that works for you.

There's also an exercise you can perform at home. Deal five hold'em hands face up and pretend that the three best hands, no matter how bad they are, will be played all the way to the river. This comes close to simulating an actual short-handed game. The more times you do this the more you will see that you can win without premium cards. This exercise will also convince you that your opponents will actually have trash most of the time and you won't have to fear every bet.

SMALL BLIND

How do I decide whether or not to call the other half of the bet when I have bad cards in the small blind?
You just answered your own question. Bad cards are bad cards in any position. The fact that you can get in for half price doesn't mean much. Here's the most important consideration: The odds against improving bad cards are far greater than any pot odds you can get for those cards before the flop. If you do have to play in the small blind, limit your calls to those times when you're suited—and you don't have to play all of those hands. Computer simulation has shown that most of the value you realize from small blind cards comes from the fact that they are suited.

I still hate to fold in the small blind. Can you come up with another good reason I should fold?
If you fold in the small blind, you win something very big—the button on the next hand.

I've heard that there's a hidden cost to playing in the small blind? Is that true?
Yes. The hidden cost is the fact that after you limp in for half a bet, you now get to lose more money on the flop,

turn and river with a hand you never would have called a full bet with before the flop.

SMOKING
Isn't it great that poker rooms are now adopting a no smoking policy?

In reality, it only helps a little bit. I know of no poker room where there's a ban on smoking in the entire building. I play at the Imperial Palace in Biloxi. The poker room is located on the third floor and the entire floor is a no smoking area. The problem is that smoking is allowed on the first and second floors of the casino and as we all know, heat, warm air, and the cigarette smoke that's in it all rise to the top. Consequently, I always go home with a smoker's cough that lasts for a day after playing eight hours or more in the "non-smoking" poker room.

SPLIT POTS
Do you have any advice on how I should play whenever I'm looking at a possible split pot?

Winston Churchill said, "Never, never, never, never give up." I want to paraphrase him and tell you to never, never, never, never assume you're going to have a split pot just because it looks like it's possible and probable. If the board is K♠ Q♣ J♦ 10♥ and you have an ace, do not assume that your opponent also has the ace-high straight just because he bets, raises or reraises you. You have absolutely nothing to lose by putting in the maximum number of bets. The worst that could happen is that you're going to split a bigger pot.

Sometimes your opponent will have a 9, for the lower end of the straight or he will have trips or two pair, hoping to make a full house on the river. If he does, then only six to ten cards will help him, which makes you a 4 to 1 or 6 to 1 favorite over him with one card to come. The situation is even better if there's a third player trying to draw out on you. You'll be a big winner in the long run if you always bet and raise with the nuts.

SUPPLIES

I have a home hold'em game that I'd like to run as professionally as possible. Do you know where I can get good decks of cards, chips, dealer button, cut cards and the other stuff that would make my game look good?

The one best source for poker supplies is the Gambler's General Store, on 800 South Main Street, in Las Vegas. You can reach them at 1-800-322-2447 or online at www.gamblersgeneralstore.com. They'll send you a giant, oversized 85-page catalogue for free.

SURVEILLANCE

Can you tell me what the surveillance cameras in the poker room can see? I tried to get invited into the surveillance control room for a look-see and they just laughed at me.

I can tell you that no one is watching you play poker. The surveillance is a passive activity because security is not really concerned with what's going on in the poker room. After all, nobody in there is getting a 5 percent edge over the casino. They don't care who wins as long as the poker room gets their rake. About the only time they ever look at a poker room surveillance tape is when there's a jackpot to be verified or a gorgeous blonde accidentally wanders into the poker room.

On a more serious note, their cameras are the best in the world. If you lay a $100 bill on the poker table, the security expert in surveillance can quickly and easily read the serial number and the name "WASHINGTON" under his portrait on the $1 bill.

The next time the dealer pushes the pot to the wrong person and the poker room manager says, "I'll call surveillance to see who actually won the pot," don't you believe it for one second when he comes back and says, "They couldn't make out the difference between a spade and a club in your hand so I'm going to have to rule that that player gets to keep the pot." Those cameras were bought, tested and installed precisely because they can tell the difference between the suits of the cards—and everything else.

TELLS
What's your favorite tell? Which one tell do you think has been worth the most money to you?
I think it's watching preflop raisers watch the flop. I don't look at the flop when the dealer turns it up—I look at the preflop raiser. The flop will still be there a few seconds later when I take a look at it. I've become good at determining if the raiser hit the flop or not. Having this much information early in the game has

been very valuable to me over the years. I have never liked to wear a hat, but this is the reason I've taken to wear a visor when I play poker. It helps conceal my eyes when I'm watching the other players so I don't tip them off that I'm so serious about the game.

Have any new tells been discovered since Mike Caro wrote his *The Body Language of Poker* book on tells back in the 1980s?
I'm aware of two tells that I've found to be useful and reliable that aren't in the book you mentioned. The first is the fact that a player who fumbles or otherwise accidentally loses control of his poker chips while he's making a bet is much more likely than usual to be bluffing. The other tell is that a player who answers a question at a critical time in the hand in a very slightly higher pitch than his usual voice is more likely to be bluffing or not telling the truth.

TIPS
How much should I tip a dealer when I win the big part of a jackpot?
To begin with, don't forget that all of the money in the jackpot belongs to the players. The dealers are not entitled to a fixed percentage of it as is commonly believed. The dealers have already been tipped for every hand they dealt while that jackpot was being built up to the amount it was when you hit it. I don't believe in educating the other players at the table, but one of the things that I do enjoy saying is, "Did you know that the deal-

ers have already been tipped more money than what is in the jackpot right now?"

For every hand that a dealer deals, he is tipped $1 (on average) and $1 is raked for the jackpot. Typically, sixty cents goes into the primary jackpot, twenty-five cents goes into the backup jackpot and fifteen cents goes into the tertiary jackpot. That means that for every dollar the dealers are tipped, only sixty cents goes into the jackpot.

When you hit the big part of the jackpot, remember that you are not in a tournament and you won this money in one hand, not over the course of a five-hour tournament. However, I think I would tip a dealer about $300 for a $10,000 jackpot, which is 3 percent, but I'd tip a smaller percentage as the jackpot got bigger.

I see this tipping question as a "philosophy versus value" dilemma. Is the guideline going to be a certain percentage or certain maximum amount of money? Would you like to tip 3 percent and then realize that $300 is too much? It's up to you. Only you can decide what you're comfortable with.

I don't like it when I'm in the game and the dealer that I've been tipping gets off work, takes a seat right next to me, and then plays against me with the very money I

gave him. It doesn't seem right, yet I know I'm probably wrong to think like this. What can I do?

In 1967 the great advice columnist Ann Landers fielded this question: "My ten-year-old son always eats all of the food I put on his dinner plate, but he has the peculiar habit of eating all of his meat at once, then the potatoes and then the vegetables. What should I do?" I'm going to give you the exact, same advice that Ann Landers gave that worried mother: "MYOB."

TOP PAIR

I've overheard other hold'em players discuss strategy and I think they were talking about folding when they flop top pair. Can this possibly be right?

I fold top pair regularly and it's one of the strategies that makes me an overall winner. Surprised? Don't be, because what I'm really doing is folding whenever I think I'm beat or can't otherwise win the hand; sometimes that will include when I'm holding top pair on the flop.

Obviously, it's the other factors that makes the fold correct. If you have K♥ 3♥ in the big blind and the flop is K♣ J♦ 10♠, you certainly don't have the best hand when there's a bet and five callers in front of you. I also save a lot of money by folding when I have ace-little and there's a lot of interest in the pot when another ace flops. It's not that I'm deliberately trying to fold top pair, it's that I'm willing to fold anytime I think it's correct to do so.

TOURNAMENTS
Is it good to be an alternate in a tournament?
Waiting until the second or even third round of a tournament to begin play is essentially the same thing as having been in the tournament all the time and not playing a hand, including having the bonus of not having had to post any blinds. Or, it's the same as having been in the seat all that time and still having the same amount of chips that you started with. Also, it's nice to be seated at the table forty minutes after the tournament started and instantly be in third place at your table.

On the other hand, the way you win tournaments (in theory, anyway) is to keep doubling up your stack of chips until you have all the chips. From this perspective the time you spend on the rail waiting to get in could be keeping you from moving up the payout ladder.

So, in my opinion, the answer is, if you're a bad hold'em tournament player, then it's good to be an alternate. If you're a good hold'em tournament player, then I think you'd prefer to not be an alternate.

What's your opinion of women's-only tournaments?
I understand why women's-only tournaments originated and have been so popular. It's because in the early days of the social acceptance of public poker, most women were intimidated by the presence of men in the game. And for good reason. The men had one heck of a lot more experience at poker than the average woman did. But the world has changed and the original reasons

that created women's-only tournaments no longer exist. There is no longer a need to separate, and therefore protect, the lady poker player in the twenty-first century.

If you want to eliminate women's-only poker tournaments for good, all you'd have to do is insist on having a men's-only tournament. There'd be an Equal Rights Poker Amendment to the Constitution in the works in very short order.

What is the "bubble?"

In a tournament, it's the first place that does not get paid. If the payout schedule calls for the top 10 places to be paid, then eleventh place is on the bubble. It's very often the difference between nothing and several hundred dollars. In the WSOP main event, it's the difference between nothing and a $10,000+ payoff.

VERY PERSONAL
What's the wildest or most memorable bet you ever won?

When I was about twenty-one years old, I had a bet with my boss that "I can name any tune you can whistle." He thought about it for a minute and then whistled a song that I had never heard of before in my life. I thought about it for a while and then said, "I'll bet that that was your college fight song." I was right and won the $20 wager. It's the best bet I ever won because of the 1,000,000 to 1 odds against me making the right guess.

WORLD SERIES OF POKER (WSOP)

Would you make any changes to the World Series of Poker, if you could?

There is one aspect of the series that I think is seriously in need of updating—and that's the buy-in for the $10,000 no-limit hold'em event that crowns the annual world champion. The buy-in was $10,000 in 1970. I think it should be adjusted for inflation and the new buy-in should be a cool $25,000. If $10,000 was alright in 1970, then $25,000 ought to be alright now, because after all, they're really the same amount of money adjusted for time.

One other thing I might change if it were up to me, is to hold the WSOP in the spring or fall instead of during the hottest days of the year in the middle of summer. The average high is 110 degrees every July in Las Vegas while the nighttime temperature doesn't drop below 100 degrees.

I would also like to see the WSOP crown a World Champion of Poker who would be recognized as the best all-around poker player in the world, instead of the best hold'em player until the next annual event. That tournament should be much like the HORSE tournament is now. Right now, the entire tournament centers around waiting to see who the $10,000 no-limit hold'em winner is going to be, and then calling him the World Champion. I don't think that's right.

There are a dozen types of poker games that are currently played. How can a champion of just one of those games be the world champion of all poker? There should be a new category of champions who we can call the best all-round poker players in the world, and that event should consist of at least all of the events in the HORSE tournaments, plus a few more like triple draw and deuce-to-seven stud.

Another thing I would change about the WSOP concerns the taping and broadcasting of the main event on the cable channels. By the time the action gets to the final few tables, there are thousands of individual poker chips distributed among the two dozen or so survivors. I think it's ridiculous for a player to have as many as one thousand poker chips in front of him. It's very difficult for the watching public to know exactly what each chip is worth and it's almost always impossible to tell how much a player is betting by looking at the chips he's cutting out of his stack.

There has to be some serious coloring-up by the time the action gets to the final table. Yeah, I know it looks good for TV, but it's impracticable and is a burden on the viewers. My solution is to make an effort to color-up to the maximum extent possible and to do one other thing: Introduce European-style poker chips at this stage of the game. They're rectangular in shape and about the size and thickness of a half-deck of cards. Make the smallest denomination rectangular chip worth a cool $1,000,000.

Why do so many former world champions and world-class players always bust out of the main event on the first day?

Don't forget that the WSOP main event is an eight- or nine-day tournament. Many of these champions are multimillionaires who could be making much more money by playing in the side games for those five days rather than making it to the fifth day and then busting out. So, they take the attitude that they're willing to risk doubling or tripling up on the first day with the knowledge that they can play in a side game if they get busted out. If they triple up on day one, then fine, they have a great advantage and the tournament is now worth playing to the end. If not, they go straight to a side game with a $100,000 or more buy-in.

Would you or are you ever going to play in the WSOP?

I don't like the idea of paying $10,000 to enter a tournament with a field of thousands. All it takes is one very good, but unlucky hand to knock you out of the tournament. With that in mind, I think I get a better value for my dollar by playing ring games and smaller buy-in tournaments.

8♠ 8♣ VERSUS 8♦ 7♦

Would you rather hold a pocket pair or suited connectors of the same pip value, such as 8-8 or 8-7 suited?

The answer is the same as almost all poker questions: It depends. 8-7 suited is a drawing hand that requires good multiway action to be profitable in the long run. It's even better if you're in late position with it. You'll win a big pot if you make a hand. The downside is that it will often cost you a lot of money to see the river card only to find out that you've missed your straight or flush draw.

I like a pair of eights because you can usually see the flop for one bet and then you're out of there if you miss and have to fold. This is the feature that makes hold'em a much better game than other forms of poker — you get to see five-sevenths of your hand for one small bet.

14.
KEN WARREN ANSWERS YOUR PERSONAL QUESTIONS

My publisher tells me that I am one of the best-selling poker writers of all time. I appreciate that. I've always believed that I've succeeded because of the fact that I'm a teacher who's trying to teach poker rather than a poker player who's trying to be a writer. My intended audience has always been the non-player and the beginning poker player. I've always looked at my job as a poker writer as trying to accomplish three goals:

1. Getting strangers to the game of poker seated at the poker table.

2. Teaching beginners as much as they need to know to learn this complicated game and to hold their own from the very beginning.

3. To write in a friendly, easy-to-read style while being interesting, entertaining and educational. I believe I've hit the mark in good fashion.

The fact that I put my email address in my poker books means that hundreds of my readers have written me asking for poker advice and surprisingly, a lot of personal questions. My mail has been about 90 percent asking about poker and about 10 percent asking about me, my life and my poker experiences. I'm going to use this chapter to answer some of the more interesting and personal questions that I've received. Some of this stuff is even true!

I'll number the questions to make it easier to refer to one if you have to write me about it.

1. How did you learn to play poker?
In 1980, I was a sergeant in the U.S. Air Force. They sent me to a remote location in Turkey where I lived in a two-man barracks room with Fermon L. "Pete" Langton, a good ole' boy from Louisiana. He appropriated the third floor's round kitchen table out of the dayroom and had a six to eight person poker game in our little room after work. The game went from 5 p.m. until well after midnight every day, while I tried to get some sleep, starting at about 10 p.m. It never worked, so after about two weeks, I decided if I couldn't beat 'em, I'd join 'em. They taught me how to play, I loved it, and twelve months later, when it was time for me to rotate back to the States, I seriously considered extending my tour just because the game was so profitable.

2. How did you get your live poker nickname and your online name?
In 1993 I stood in a long line to register for a hold'em tournament at Casino Magic in Bay St. Louis, Mississippi. When it was my turn, I told them my name was Ken and the registration attendant said, "We already have five Kens; do you have a nickname?" I didn't, but I immediately

recalled that poker saying about never play poker with a guy named after a city or a guy named "Doc." So, I said, "Yeah. My nickname is Doc," and from that time on everyone on the Mississippi Gulf Coast poker scene knew me only as Doc and not as Ken.

3. What's the biggest pot you've ever won at limit poker?

I was in a $20/$40 hold'em game at the Golden Nugget in 1985. I held 7♣ 7♠ and the betting was capped with one bet and four raises with seven-way action to see the flop. There was already $700 in the pot before the flop. The flop was A♥ K♦ 7♥. The betting was capped again. The turn was the 6♦, the betting was capped once again, and we lost one player. The river was the 2♥, the betting was capped, and now there were just four of us left. I was pretty sure I was looking at a set of aces or kings, but I couldn't let the hand go.

I almost couldn't believe it when the first player proudly turned over A-K, as did the second and third player! The pot was about $3,600.

4. What's the biggest pot you've ever won at no-limit?

I don't play much no-limit, but I do have one big win. I was in a game at the Gulfport Grand. I held J♠ J♦ and the flop was J♣ 7♦ 7♥. One player held the case jack and two other players each flopped three sevens. The pot was about $7,000.

5. What's your biggest loss at poker?

One of the first times I ever player pot-limit Omaha, I flopped aces-full (A-A-A-3-3). I lost on the river when the other player spiked a 9 to make a higher full house. That hand cost me $1,000.

The worst loss I ever had, emotionally speaking, was when I sat down in a $10/$20 hold'em game at the Stardust in 1985. I handed the chip runner my $500 buy-in for a rack of red and the dealer dealt me in. I said, "I'm raising," and he gave me $500 out of his dealer's rack to play with. I had pocket aces and I lost half my stack in that hand.

The very next hand I was dealt K♣ K♠ and I flopped another king. I then proceeded to lose the other half of my stack when I got beat by a straight on the river. I was all-in and lost. Just as the dealer is pushing the pot to the winner, the chip runner arrives with my rack of red. Since it was all of the money that I had to play with at that time, I had to give the rack to the dealer, get up and leave the game. I still hate that memory after twenty-three years.

Another time, I was in a game at the Commerce in Los Angeles in 1989. The jackpot was an even $10,000 and at that time, it was split 80/20 between the winner and the loser of the jackpot hand. I was dealt A♠ A♥ and my opponent was dealt K♦ K♥. The flop was A♣ K♠ K♣! I knew instantly that if he had four kings, we had a jackpot and I was going to win $8,000. Well, the turn was the 5♥ and the river was A♦. Instead of losing the hand with aces full of kings, I won the hand with four aces!

I got the winner's share instead of the loser's share, but the A♦ on the river cost me $6,000.

Here's a third story. I was in a hold'em game at the Boomtown Casino in Biloxi in 2007. Just as I looked down and saw J♦ J♣, my phone began to ring. I called a raise to see the flop as my phone kept ringing. The flop was A♠ A♣ 5♦ and I folded my hand to answer my phone—the caller ID showed that it was my wife. The turn card was the 7♦ and the river was the A♥. I would have won half of a $17,852 jackpot if my phone had not rung exactly when it did. (And no, the call was not important.)

I saved my worst loss for last. I was in a hold'em game at the Biloxi Grand in 1996. The jackpot was $96,000. I made four deuces and lost to four queens. I was going to get $48,000 in cash if everything worked out alright. It didn't. The player with the four queens turned out to be underage. The hand was ruled to be null and void from its inception and everyone got their money back.

6. How did you meet your wife? Is she a poker player?
I used to drive an 18-wheeler all over the country, going from poker room to poker room. The company I worked for knew I was a player and writer and they didn't care if I played poker as long as I picked up and delivered on time and didn't drive out of route. One night, I arrived

at the Kansas City Ameristar Casino and signed up at the poker room. They told me I was #7 on the list and I'd be called. So, I went down to the keno machine and took a seat. I struck up a conversation with the woman sitting beside me and after about three hours, I was called for my poker seat.

I left the next morning, drove to Baltimore, Houston, Los Angeles, Salt Lake City and then back to Kansas City two weeks after I had left. I signed up at the poker room and was put on the list. While waiting, I went back to the same keno machine I was at two weeks earlier. The same woman was still sitting at the same machine! We got married about six months later.

Olga knew absolutely nothing about poker. I taught her how to play and she won $100 the first time she ever played in a poker room.

7. Do you have any poker stories from Biloxi, Mississippi?

I moved to Biloxi in September, 1990. At that time, it was one of the poorest and most poverty stricken cities in the U.S. Except for the military base there, there was almost no local economy, save for the port of Gulfport and some local fishing. It seemed that most people were either retired military, or living on food stamps and government welfare. The most successful businesses in town were the pawn shops. Almost every business closed by 5 p.m. and only the mall was open on Sunday, and usually was not very busy at all.

The initiative to approve casino-style gambling had been on the ballot in March of 1988, 1989, 1990 and 1991. It was soundly defeated every time because Biloxi is smack in the middle of the Bible Belt and the evils of gambling were taught in all the local churches.

But something happened in the summer of 1991 to change all that. The big corporations that own the big casinos flew in hundreds of casino executives and ad men into the Biloxi area to have face-to-face meetings with the local religious leadership. They explained to them that casinos would provide jobs that would raise the whole local economy out of poverty, everyone would enjoy a higher standard of living, and a substantial portion of the gaming revenue would go to the state for education and infrastructure improvements. And most important of all, the preachers were made to understand that the average parishioner would then have much more money to put in the collection plate on Sunday.

The gambling initiative passed overwhelmingly on March 15th, 1992. The first casino opened in Biloxi three months later and I won the first hand of legal poker dealt in the state of Mississippi in the twentieth century.

I had found a home game where I could play on Friday and Saturday nights. I lived in Ocean Springs and the game was in Gulfport, about ten miles away. The most amazing thing about my time playing in this home game was the fact that when I left the house at 6 p.m. and made the ten mile drive down Highway 90 (the

Gulf Coast Highway), there was not once, ever, another car on the road. Unbelievable. That's a sign of how economically dead the town was. I didn't even pass a police car making the rounds. And that certainly held true for my trip back home sometime after midnight.

The first thing that happened when the President Casino opened their poker room was that every local player within one hundred miles came in to play. And because of that, every card in the deck had deep thumbnail marks in them because, well, it looked to me that everyone was cheating by marking the cards. They actually had to go through a dozen decks in one day to keep the cards unmarked. That practice eventually died out when everyone realized what a casino poker room was.

I remember that dealers had to be trained from scratch, because they knew nothing about how to deal or even what beats what in poker. I remember they used to tell the players that they had the "high" and the "low" blinds when it was their turn. And I remember the floorperson telling players that they could not leave the table to go eat until the other player returned from his dinner. They also told players that once they got into their game, they were not allowed to move up in limit if their absence would make their current game short-handed. Imagine that! It was pretty much an amateurish operation in the beginning.

The most ridiculous thing that I ever saw was some of the female dealers trying to shuffle and deal with two- and three-inch painted nails. It didn't work and they refused to cut them for a long time.

The first time I had to shake my head in laughter was when I heard on the news that a driver on the freeway (Interstate 10) had reported to the Mississippi Highway Patrol that two men were dropping a washing machine off the overpass onto the freeway below in the middle of the night. It turned out to be an ATM machine stolen from the Gulfport Grand Casino!

And then, about a year later, seven security guards who worked at the Gulfport Grand robbed the place for a lot of money. That part made the news. After that, nothing made the news. The story just went away and no one at the Grand would talk about it. I suspect they made a deal with the guards to get the money back in exchange for dropping the charges and they didn't want that to be known, if it was true. I don't know.

8. What's the most statistically unlikely thing you've ever seen at the poker table?

I was in a hold'em game at the Biloxi Belle in 1995 where five players all showed their hole cards at the end. Every one of them had a set! They all started with a pocket pair, three of them flopped a set, the fourth player got his set on the turn and the fifth player got his set on the river.

Another time, I was in a game at the Isle of Capri in Biloxi in 2007 and was dealt pocket kings—only the second king had flashed when the dealer threw it towards me. He had to take it back and give me a replacement card. It was another king! I then proceeded to get the case king on the flop. I won the hand—no harm, no foul.

9. What's the weirdest hand you've ever won?
I was in a $10/$20 hold'em game at the Stardust in 1988. On the river, there was about $400 in the pot and the first player said, "Bet." The second player folded as did the third, fourth and fifth players. It was left to me, the last player. As much as I wanted to call that bet, I couldn't because I had absolutely nothing and couldn't even beat a bluff. So I mucked my hand and let the pot go.

It turned out that the player who said, "Bet," was a joker who was just fooling around and he didn't even have any cards. The floorman was called and he ruled that since I was the last active player to have a hand, I won the pot. So, I won a $400 pot with no cards!

10. Has another player ever physically threatened you during a poker game?
One time during an all-night hold'em game at the Stardust, I told a very funny, but off-color joke and another player at the table scolded me with, "My wife's here at the table. Watch your language." Well, I didn't mean to offend anybody so I shut up for a while. I forgot about it and just naturally told another joke a little bit later.

The same guy said, "I'm warning you—watch your language at the table!" Well that really challenged me. About thirty minutes later I told another joke and he said, "Alright, I've had it with you, I'll be waiting for you outside." And he and his wife left.

I played for about another four hours, knowing no one would wait around like that for real. I cashed out and left the building and to my shock and horror—there he was standing outside the door with a razor in his hand!! And if he'd had a place to plug it in....

11. What's your favorite story to tell at the poker table?

I love to tell this story at the poker table because it's genuinely hilarious and the listener likes it because he realizes that I got one over on him.

In almost every game I play in, in any part of the country, there are always retired military veterans and first-generation Americans from Vietnam, Laos, Cambodia and Thailand. Inevitably, I'd be able to steer the conversation around to the Vietnam War where I casually and nonchalantly worked in the comment, "If it wasn't for the war, I wouldn't have met my wife."

I would then go on to say, "It's the best thing that ever happened to me. I got to see a foreign country, learn a new language, new culture, totally different lifestyle, new foods, and I made friends that will last a lifetime." And while I'm saying this and dragging it out for effect,

I can see the players from Southeast Asia slowly start to sit up in their chairs, start to beam with pride and then when I'm finished talking, one of them would proudly ask, "Oh, is your wife Vietnamese?"

And I answer in my best straight-faced, deadpan manner, "No, she's Canadian." Whereupon, everyone at the table over the age of 50 has to take five minutes out of the game to laugh uncontrollably, clear the tears from their eyes and then explain it to everybody at the table under the age of 50.

(Okay, for you readers under the age of 50, Vietnam War-era draft dodgers fled to Canada so they wouldn't have to serve in the war. Jimmy Carter's very first act as President of the United States was to pardon all of them.)

12. What lines or quotes do you want to be remembered for?
When I was working on my first book, *Winner's Guide to Texas Hold'em Poker,* I came to realize that position at the hold'em table is just as important as location is when selling real estate. So I said, "What they say about the three most important things in real estate—location, location and location—are just as true at hold'em: position, position and position." There's another poker writer and speaker out there who uses that quote extensively, but I said it first in 1996—in writing.

When I was working on a chapter on cheating at poker for my *Big Book of Poker,* I summarized it by saying

"Poker is not a team sport." Here are some of my other favorite self-penned quotes:

> "If you can't be an honest poker player, then you should just be honest without being a poker player."

> My philosophy of money management is summed up by "No style, type or form of money management will work if you play a game of skill without the skill."

> Once during a hold'em game I actually asked everyone at the table, "Have you ever prayed for eternal salvation as hard as you've prayed for a club on the river?"

> "If you want to be a professional poker player, there is no elevator to the top. You have to take the stairs."

> "All I want is a fair advantage."

> "I want this game to be fair, but not so fair that I could lose."

> "The true purpose of poker-playing should be to improve the well-being of your family."

ODDS AND ENDS

Here are some odds and ends I thought I would include to finish out the book.

My goal is to make you a $10/$20 player

My purpose as a poker writer, and my goal, is to teach beginners how to play and not be a loser from the start. But the truth is, if you stick to just the very lowest limit, you'll really be wasting a lot of time and for not very much money. However, if you can move up to $10/$20 (you can), you'll have a much better lifetime poker experience.

If you're currently a $2/$4 or $3/$6 player, I want to assure you that you are capable of moving up to $10/$20. If you currently buy in for a rack of white ($1) chips, you can buy in for a rack of red ($5) and still play "$2/$4," only it will be red chips. The rake will be a much smaller percentage of each pot, the players aren't any better, thanks to the explosion in the popularity of poker, and besides, if you're good enough to double your buy-in, wouldn't you rather be cashing two racks of red rather than white chips?

I am a poker historian

I'm a serious student of history. I used to teach U.S. history and U.S. government at Arizona State University. In the process of learning, teaching and writing about poker, I became interested in its history. I was the first poker writer to publish a timeline of the history of playing cards and poker (*Big Book of Poker*). If you know some interesting poker history, maybe you could share it with me.

I like to travel

I'm willing to come to your town to meet you. If you'd like me to appear in your poker room, give you private lessons, conduct a poker seminar or teach a class, I'm your guy. No location on the planet is out of the question. If you'll cover the cost of travel and other expenses, we can make a deal.

Email

I have my area of poker specialization. You just read it. As much as I appreciate getting email from my readers, I'd like to ask that you don't send me questions about playing online and no-limit poker. On those topics, other poker writers could be much more help to you than I could. Thanks. My personal email is kennolga@yahoo.com.

15.
LAST WORD

I hope you got a lot of helpful and winning information out of this book and enjoyed reading the concepts and ideas as much as I enjoyed writing them. I've written some other books you may enjoy as well, listed below. You can contact my publisher directly if you'd like to obtain copies of these.

- Winner's Guide to Texas Hold'em Poker

- Ken Warren Teaches Texas Hold'em (Volume I)

- Ken Warren Teaches Texas Hold'em (Volume II)

- Ken Warren Teaches 7-Card Stud

- Winners Guide to Omaha Poker

- The Big Book of Poker

You can order these from Cardoza Publishing by phone (800)577-WINS or (702)870-7200, or through their website: www.cardozabooks.com.

APPENDIX:
ACES CRACKED!

There's a promotion being introduced in the brick and mortar poker rooms around the country that's gaining traction. It's called "Aces Cracked." That means a player who is dealt pocket aces and then loses with the hand is given $100 in poker chips for free from the poker room's cashier. It's a gift—all you have to do is lose with two aces in your hand. When you look at your hand and you see A♣ A♥, you instantly know that one of two things is going to happen: You're either going to win the hand or you're going to win $100. This giveaway has the effect of insuring pocket aces against a loss.

It's a great promotion—and is liked by both poker room managers and players alike—but it has created a weird situation where players are now trying to deliberately lose the hand when they hold pocket aces because the $100 reward for losing is usually much more than your net win if you win the pot in a low-limit game. This means that for this one hand only, the object of the game has changed. The real object of the game of poker is, and always has been, to make the best decisions you can with the information available to you at the time and then, as they say, "Let the chips fall where they may."

When you look down and see A♠ A♦, the object of the game has changed to one of trying to make the most amount of money you can on this hand—one way or the other. This calls for careful analysis of the situation and that, in turn, reveals that there are some strategy changes to be made if you're going to get the most money you can out of this hand. You just can't play A♣ A♦ the same way you always play them. It might cost you a lot of money.

Let's look at this situation by starting with what we already know about pocket aces before the flop:

- It's 220 to 1 against being dealt pocket aces

- That means in an eight-hour playing session where you get 35 hands per hour, you'll be dealt pocket aces once, perhaps twice if you're lucky during that session

- That means that *someone else* at your table will be dealt pocket aces about eleven or twelve times on average

- You are about a 4 to 1 favorite over just one opponent if you both play to the river

- You will flop another ace about one out of eight times

- You will flop a full house about 1 percent of the time

Now you know where you stand with pocket aces. If you're in a tight, no-action game and the pots are small, you have a lot to gain just by checking and calling all the way to the river, hoping to be beat. If the game is wild and crazy and the pots are huge, then you might not have that much to gain from the promotion, since it appears you will probably win $100 anyway, whether you win or lose the hand.

Here's some strategy changes and considerations you should be aware of before you're even dealt the cards:

- You're going to win a certain amount of the time with pocket aces, no matter how hard you try to lose with them. Try to learn to recognize those types of flops that mean you're going to win.

- Once you see A♣ A♥ in your hand, it's a balancing act between trying to make the pot as big as possible if you're going to win, and spending as little as possible of that $100 if you're going to lose the hand.

- Why should you even play in the game if you're only going to get pocket aces once a day? And then you still might win with the hand and the $100 promotion wouldn't apply to you anyway? The answer is that your real profit in this promotion comes from the fact your opponents will get pocket aces a dozen times a day while playing against you, and they will do everything they can to help you beat them.

- There is less preflop raising during an aces cracked promotion. You're going to be able to limp in more often with slightly weaker hands because you know you won't be raised as often. You will not be punished for trying to draw out on a player holding pocket aces.

- If there is a preflop raise, you know the raiser most likely has A♣ K♥, K♣ K♦ or Q♠ Q♦ and not pocket aces. This makes the hand easier to read as it progresses.

- This makes the jackpot a little easier to hit. Players holding pocket kings, queens and jacks won't be run off as often.

- There should be a rule against chopping for the time the promotion is in effect. One-fifth of the time that aces are dealt at the table, one of the blinds will be holding them. It's unfair to force a player to reveal his hand by turning down a request to chop.

- Unless there's some wild players in the game, the promotion tends to keep the pots smaller than average. That's because there's less raising before the flop which means there's less reraising before the flop.

- If the game is short-handed, you should realize that you're going to win a lot more often than not. You should probably let everyone in to see the flop and then go ahead and play your usual strategy for the rest of the hand unless a flare goes off, indicating that you're going to lose the hand.

- Ordinarily, the number of players against you is the most important factor in determining your chances of winning or losing a hand. However, when playing aces cracked, you have to pay a lot more attention to *the texture of the flop* than you did before. This will be a more accurate indicator of your chances of winning the hand.

- You can play A-X a little more liberally than usual because the player holding A♣ A♥ will not make you pay for the fact that you have an inferior hand before the flop, as he should.

- You can call a preflop raise with A-X a little more liberally because the raiser likely doesn't have pocket aces.

- What if you hold pocket aces and you have to call a preflop raise? If there are a lot of players in the hand, you probably don't want to reraise and risk driving out players who might end up beating you. On the other hand, if you feel you can reraise without driving anyone out, you should probably do so. Look at it as taking some of that $100 and using it to build the pot you might win. After all, you are the favorite at this point.

- Believe it or not, there are two times when it's correct to raise before the flop with pocket aces. The first is when you're heads-up and it's obvious that this guy is not going to fold. Go ahead and raise, because you're going to win this hand about 80 percent of the time. Get all the money you can from him. If he happens to win the hand, you still get the $100 minus an extra bet or two that you got in.

- The other time to raise preflop is if you're in late position, there are a lot of callers already in the pot, and (here's the really important part) a raise from you will not force anyone to fold. As a matter of fact, you should raise if you think it will cause someone else to reraise without losing anyone before the flop. Before reading further, can you see why?

It's because having a huge pot on the flop actually increases your chances of losing the hand! A large pot makes it mathematically correct for players who have long-shot draws to keep playing. A player who flops a small pair or a three-flush or a three-straight will have to fold when the pot is small. But if the pot is really big, it's more tempting for them to call a small bet on the flop to try to improve their draw on the turn. In other words, a big pot on the flop encourages more players to try to run you down with all kinds of hands. And that's what you want.

You should always pause and take a little bit more time than usual to think about your hand after the river card hits the board. That card decides your fate, but you have to figure out how. There will be times that it's obvious you're going to either win or lose the hand. It's those average, middle strength hands in between that have the potential for saving or losing an extra bet.

Bet most hands that you think you'll win. You're insured if you're wrong. I always bet against one or two players who check to me on the river. I'm willing to risk a small part of the $100 to win an extra bet or two on the end. I would also say you should bet most hands that you're not sure of. Again, you'll either win extra bets or lose only one bet out of the promotion money.

How much is the aces cracked promotion theoretically worth to you in one eight-hour session?

An exact amount is not possible to compute because it depends on the average pot size, how your opponents play, and how you play when you get the pocket aces. My answer to that question might surprise you: Most of the profit you realize comes to you when the other players, and not you, have the pocket aces. That's because you will be in the hand to win an extra pot or two that you would not have won had the holder of the pocket aces correctly tried to run you out. And when you do lose a hand to pocket aces, it will almost always have cost you less to play that hand rather than more.

These small edges add up and are valuable to you, especially if you know about them in advance. And now you do.

I really like the aces cracked promotion. It's a little easier to win a little more money when it's going on. But as a poker purist, it bothers me a little that a promotion would cause good players to deviate from the true spirit of the game and play incorrectly for the purpose of winning a side bet.

GLOSSARY

A-X suited In hold'em, an ace and another card of the same suit.

Active hand A hand that is still live, the holder of which is still in contention for the pot.

Add on In a tournament, the last additional chips that a player may buy, usually at the break.

Ajax A-J as pocket cards.

All in The act of putting all the remaining chips you have in the pot, usually before the hand is over. A player who is all in can win only that part of the pot he was able to match if he has the best hand at the end.

American Airlines Pocket aces.

B & M Stands for "bricks and mortar." Used to describe poker rooms that actually exist in buildings, as opposed to online poker rooms that exist only in cyberspace.

Backdoor Making a hand that you originally weren't drawing to or trying to make. For example, you hold A♥ J♥ in hold'em and the flop is Q♥ 7♥ 3♦ and the turn is the K♦ and the river is the 10♠, giving you the nut straight, even though you were hoping for the heart flush after the flop.

Backraise	A reraise from a player who originally just called on that round.
Bad beat	To lose with a great hand — usually aces full or better — to a player who made a longshot draw.
Banker	Usually applies only to home games. The one player who is responsible for selling the poker chips, keeping the cash, possibly providing credit, and keeping the bookwork and accounting straight for that game.
Bankroll	The money you have set aside to put into a poker game. This money is physically, or at least mentally, segregated from other money used for non-playing expenses.
Baskin Robbins	3-A as pocket cards (31 flavors).
Beer hand	7-2 as pocket cards. The worst starting hand in hold'em.

Big blind	The bigger of two blinds in a game; a mandatory bet posted by the player two places to the dealer's left.
Big flop	A flop that gives you a powerful hand.
Big slick	A-K as pocket cards.
Black chip	A $100 poker chip.
Blank	A card that is of no apparent help to a poker hand. Also called a *brick*.
Bluff	To bet with a hand that is likely to lose if called.
Board	The cards that are turned face up in a flop game and belong to everyone. Also called *community cards*.
Boxed card	A card that is accidentally turned face up during the shuffle and is then dealt to a player when it should be face down. It is treated as a blank piece of paper and is replaced with a new card after the deal is completed for that round.
Brett Maverick	J-Q as pocket cards or jacks and queens.

Broadway	An ace-high straight: A♥ K♦ Q♠ J♣ 10♦.
Broderick Crawford	10-4 as pocket cards.
Bubble	In a tournament, the last player to bust out who does not make the payout ladder and does not get paid anything. In a tournament where ten places are paid, the eleventh player is the bubble.
Bullets	Aces.
Burn or Burn card	After the deal and before each betting round, the top card, which is mucked by the dealer. This is done to protect everyone in the event the top card is marked or is somehow known to one player.
Button	In casino poker games, a round, plastic disc with the word "Dealer" printed on both sides. It's used to indicate the dealer position and moves clockwise one position after each hand is completed.
Buy-in	The amount of money that it costs to take a seat in a live game or a tournament. The live game

minimum buy-in is customarily ten times the amount of the small bet. The minimum buy-in in a $3/$6 hold'em game is $30.

Call

To match another player's bet without raising.

Calling station

A player who calls way too much when folding or raising might be a better option.

Canine

K-9 as pocket cards.

Cards speak

The concept that your poker hand is determined by what your cards actually are and not by any remarks that a player might make about his hand. All casino games are played cards speak, and if you turn your hand face up at the end of the hand, the dealer will read the hand for you.

Case card

The last card of a particular rank that has not been seen during the hand and is believed to still be in the deck.

Change gears

To change your playing style from tight to loose, or from passive to aggressive, or vice versa.

Chasing

Calling bets in an attempt to make hands that are longshot

	draws or probable losers if made.
Check	To not make a bet when it is your turn. It means, "I bet nothing." Checking is not allowed if there has been a bet in front of you.
Check-raise	To not bet initially on a round, and then to raise when there's a bet and the action gets back to you.
Chopping	When everyone but the two blinds have folded before the flop, chopping is an agreement they make to take their blinds back and end the hand right there, thus avoiding the rake.
Cold call	To call two or more bets at the same time, as opposed to calling one bet and then calling another one.
Community cards	See *board*.
Completed hand	A hand that requires all five cards to make the hand. That would be a straight, a flush, a full house, four of a kind and a straight flush.
Computer hand	Q-7 as pocket cards.
Counterfeited	To have your hand or one of

your cards nullified by a card on the board. For example, you hold A♦ 2♦ and the board is A♠ 2♥ 8♣ 5♦ 8♥. You flopped two pair but the 8♥ on the river counterfeited your hand, turning a probable loser into a losing hand or a split pot.

Cowboys	K-K as pocket cards.
Crabs	3-3 as pocket cards.
Dominated hand	A hand that nearly always loses when competing against another particular hand. Examples are higher pocket pairs versus lower pocket pairs or A-K against A-X. Dominated hands are 4-1 underdogs heads-up.
Double belly buster	A straight draw that has eight outs, yet is not an open-end straight draw. For example, you have 8-6 and the board is 10-7-4-3 with one card to come. A draw of a 9 or a 5 will make your straight.
Doyle Brunson	10-2 as pocket cards.
Draw light	When you run out of money and instead of going all-in, you play on credit. The amount of credit

is indicated by how much money or chips you have in front of you. For example, when $2 is bet, you take $2 out of the pot. At the end of the hand, the amount of money you have in front of you is what you owe the pot (if you lost the hand).

Drawing dead	Trying to make a particular hand that, even if you make it, is already beaten or cannot possibly win.
Ducks	Two deuces. Three ducks are called Huey, Duey and Louis. Four ducks are called Huey, Duey, Louis,and Uncle Donald.
Early position	To be in the first third of the players in a poker game to act on their hands.
End	The fifth, and last, community card in hold'em. Also called the *river*.
Fifth street	The fifth community card in hold'em; the river.
Flop	The first three community cards turned face up in flop games.
Flop a set	To have a pair in the pocket and to get one more of that rank on

the flop to make three of a kind, or trips.

Flush	A poker hand with five cards of the same suit that is not a straight flush or a royal flush.
Flush card	A card of the suit that you need to make your flush or to pick up a flush draw.
Flush draw	To have four cards to a flush with one or more cards to come.
Fold	To throw your hand in the discard pile, or the muck, and to forfeit all interest or claims in the pot for that hand. A verbal declaration of your intend to fold, if made in turn, is binding.
Four of a kind	A hand with four cards of the same rank. For example, 7♠ 7♦ 7♣ 7♥ K♦.
Fourth street	The fourth community card in hold'em.
Free card	A card received on a betting round where there turned out to be no bet because everyone checked.
Full	Refers to full houses. You are said to be full of whatever your three

of a kind is. J♥ J♠ J♦ 5♣ 5♠ is called "jacks full of fives."

Green chip	A $25 poker chip.
Gutshot	An inside straight draw. For example, you hold K♣ Q♥ and the flop is 10♦ 9♠ 5♥.
Heads-up	A game or betting round with only two players.
Heinz	5-7 as pocket cards.
Implied odds	Money that is not yet in the pot but you believe will be in the pot before the hand is over.
HORSE	A game or tournament with alternating rounds of hold'em, Omaha, razz, 7-card stud and 7-card stud, high-low 8 or better.
Idiot end	The low end of a straight or straight draw.
Jack Benny	3-9 as pocket cards.
Jesse James	4-5 as pocket cards.
Kicker	The highest card in your hand that does not help make a pair, straight, flush or a full house.
Kill game	A game where the betting limits are increased — usually doubled — for the next hand only.

Kojak	K♠ J♣
Late position	To be one of the last third of the players in the game to act on your hand.
Limp in	To call another player's bet (as opposed to raising).
Little blind	The smaller of two blinds in hold'em, posted by the first player to the dealer's left before the hand is dealt.
Little Oldsmobile	8-8 as pocket cards.
Live cards	Cards that you need to improve your hand and have not yet been seen.
Marriage	K♥ Q♥ as pocket cards.
Middle position	To have approximately an equal number of players before you and after you in the play of a hand.
Montana banana	2-9 as pocket cards.
Muck	To fold or throw your hand into the discard pile; the discard pile itself.
No-limit	A poker game where the players may bet any amount of money that they have in the game whenever it is their turn to play.
Off Broadway	A king-high straight: K♥ Q♠ J♦

10♣ 9♦.

Oldsmobile	9-8 as pocket cards.
On the button	To be in the dealer's position and, therefore, last to act on each betting round of that game.
Outs	The number of cards that will help your hand. For example, you have two hearts and you get two more on the flop. You have nine outs (nine hearts) that will make your hand.
Overcall	A call made after there has already been a bet and a call.
Overcard	A card on the board that is higher than either of your hole cards.
Overlay	Pot odds that are greater than the mathematical chances of making your hand.
Overpair	A pair in your hand that is higher than any card on the board. Q♠ Q♥ is an overpair if the flop is J♥ 8♣ 4♦.
Overs, Playing the	An agreement among any players in the game who want to raise the limit when only they are left in the hand.

Padding the odds	Requiring odds that are greater than the mathematical chances of making your hand.
Paint	Face cards (jacks, queens, kings).
Pocket Cards	In flop games, the first two cards you're dealt that constitute your private hand.
Pot-limit	A betting structure in which the players can only bet as much as is in the pot when it is their turn to bet.
Pot odds	The ratio of the amount of money in the pot compared to the amount of money that it cost to call a bet. For example, if the pot contains $42 and it cost you $3 to call, you're getting pot odds of 14 to 1 (42/3 = 14). If it costs you $6 to call, you're getting 7 to 1 (42/6 = 7).
Protected pot	A pot that is so huge that it's virtually certain that any bet made on the end will be called, just because of the size of the pot.
Quint	Q-10 as pocket cards.
Rabbit hunting	Asking to see what the next card would have been after the hand is over.

Rag — A card that doesn't appears to have helped anyone. Usually a low card. See *blank* and *brick*.

Rainbow flop — A flop with three different suits and no pair.

Raising in the dark — Raising before the next round, and after the current round of cards are dealt.

Raquel Welch — 3-8 as pocket cards.

Red chip — A $5 poker chip, also called a *redbird*.

Represent — To play your hand is such a way that it's obvious what you have — except you don't have that hand.

Ring game — A poker game where the buy-in and stakes are for cash. Not a tournament.

River — The fifth community card. Also called *end*.

Rock — A poker player who plays only premium starting hands.

Royal flush — An ace-high straight that is also a flush: A♦ K♦ Q♦ J♦ 10♦. There are only four of them, one for each suit. It is the highest poker hand in hold'em.

Runner-runner	Used to describe the turn and river cards when they are exactly what are needed to make a hand. Also called "perfect-perfect." Usually describes a backdoor flush draw or a double gutshot straight draw.
Rush	Winning a lot of pots close together in a short amount of time.
San Francisco busboy	Q-3 as pocket cards.
Satellite	A one-table mini-tournament where the combined buy-in of all the players is exactly the buy-in needed for a larger tournament. For example, the buy-in for the WSOP no-limit hold'em event is $10,000. You can win that buy-in by playing in and winning a satellite where ten players put up $1,000 apiece.
Semi-Bluffing	Betting with a hand that, if called, probably isn't the best hand at the moment, but has a chance to improve to the best hand by the end.
Set	The exact situation of having a pair in the pocket and flopping one more of that rank to make trips.

Sheriff	A player who likes to call on the river so that no one can get away with bluffing.
Side pot	A secondary pot that is created when one player is all in. The all-in player cannot win any of the money in a side pot.
Sit & go	A tournament that begins as soon as the minimum number of players have signed up. There is no scheduled beginning time.
Slowplay	To play your hand in a much weaker manner than its strength would usually call for in order to disguise its strength.
Snowmen	8-8 as pocket cards.
Spread-limit	A betting structure that allows you to bet any amount between the lowest and highest preset amounts.
Steal	To raise on the first round of betting with weak cards for the purpose of winning the blinds.
Straddle	Occurs when the first player after the big blind raises before he receives his cards. It does not count against the maximum number of raises limit.

Straight	A hand with five cards in sequence: A-2-3-4-5 through 10-J-Q-K-A.
Straight draw	To have four cards to a straight with one or more cards to come.
Structured limit	A betting structure that forces you to bet only the amount specified for the small bet and the big bet. It's usually a 1 to 2 ratio.
Suited connectors	Two consecutive cards of the same suit, like K♣ Q♣, 9♦ 8♦ or 6♠ 5♠.
Tell	A mannerism from an opponent that helps you figure out what his poker hand is. That mannerism can be either verbal, nonverbal, or both.
Three of a kind	A hand of three cards of the same rank and two other cards of different ranks: 8♠ 8♦ 8♣ 5♥ 2♦.
Turn	In flop games, the fourth community card.
Twiggy	2-9 as pocket cards.
Two pair	A hand with two cards of a matching rank and two other cards of a different matching rank.
Under the gun	First to act after the big blind.

Union Oil	7-6 as pocket cards.
-Up	Used to indicate two pair. A♥ A♦ 9♠ 9♣ 6♦ would be called aces-up.
White chip	A $1 poker chip.
Woolworth	5-10 as pocket cards.
World Series of Poker	A group of approximately fifty-five (as of 2008) tournaments held annually in Las Vegas. The winner of each event is crowned the World Champion in that event until the next WSOP

GREAT CARDOZA POKER BOOKS
ADD THESE TO YOUR LIBRARY - ORDER NOW!

DANIEL NEGREANU'S POWER HOLD'EM STRATEGY by *Daniel Negreanu*. This power-packed book on beating no-limit hold'em is one of the three most influential poker books ever written. Negreanu headlines a collection of young great players—Todd Brunson, David Williams. Erick Lindgren, Evelyn Ng and Paul Wasicka—who share their insider professional moves and winning secrets. You'll learn about short-handed and heads-up play, high-limit cash games, a powerful beginner's strategy to neutralize professional players, and how to mix up your play and bluff and win big pots. The centerpiece, however, is Negreanu's powerful and revolutionary small ball strategy. You'll learn how to play hold'em with cards you never would have played before—and with fantastic results. The preflop, flop, turn and river will never look the same again. A must-have! 520 pages, $34.95.

HOLD'EM WISDOM FOR ALL PLAYERS *By Daniel Negreanu*. Superstar poker player Daniel Negreanu provides 50 easy-to-read and right-to-the-point hold'em strategy nuggets that will immediately make you a better player at cash games and tournaments. His wit and wisdom makes for great reading; even better, it makes for killer winning advice. Conversational, straightforward, and educational, this book covers topics as diverse as the top 10 rookie mistakes to bullying bullies and exploiting your table image. 176 pages, $14.95.

POKER WIZARDS by *Warwick Dunnett*. In the tradition of Super System, an exclusive collection of champions and superstars have been brought together to share their strategies, insights, and tactics for winning big money at poker, specifically no-limit hold'em tournaments. This is priceless advice from players who individually have each made millions of dollars in tournaments, and collectively, have won more than 20 WSOP bracelets, two WSOP main events, 100 major tournaments and $50 million in tournament winnings! Featuring Daniel Negreanu, Dan Harrington, Marcel Luske, Kathy Liebert, Mike Sexton, Mel Judah, Marc Salem, T.J. Cloutier and Chris "Jesus" Ferguson. This must-read book is a goldmine for serious players, aspiring pros, and future champions! 352 pgs, $19.95.

MILLION DOLLAR HOLD'EM: Winning Big in Limit Cash Games by *Johnny Chan and Mark Karowe*. Learn how to win money consistently at limit hold'em, poker's most popular cash game, from one of poker's living legends. You'll get a rare opportunity to get into the mind of the man who has won ten World Series of Poker titles—tied for the most ever with Doyle Brunson—as Johnny picks out illustrative hands and shows how he thinks his way through the betting and the bluffing. No book so thoroughly details the thought process of how a hand is played, the alternative ways it could have been played, and the best way to win session after session. *Essential* reading for cash players. 400 pages, $29.95.

TOURNAMENT TIPS FROM THE POKER PROS by *Shane Smith*. Essential advice from poker theorists, authors, and tournament winners on the best strategies for winning the big prizes at low-limit rebuy tournaments. Learn proven strategies for each of the four stages of play—opening, middle, late and final—how to avoid 26 potential traps, advice on rebuys, aggressive play, clock-watching, inside moves, top 20 tips for winning tournaments, more. Advice from Brunson, McEvoy, Cloutier, Caro, Malmuth, others. 160 pages, $14.95.

NO-LIMIT TEXAS HOLD'EM: The New Player's Guide to Winning Poker's Biggest Game by *Brad Daugherty & Tom McEvoy*. For experienced limit players who want to play no limit or rookies who has never played before, two world champions show readers how to evaluate the strength of a hand, determine the amount to bet, understand opponents' play, plus how to bluff and when to do it. Seventy-four game scenarios, unique betting charts for tournament play, and sections on essential principles and strategies show you how to get to the winner's circle. Special section on beating online tournaments. 288 pages, $24.95.

GREAT CARDOZA POKER BOOKS
ADD THESE TO YOUR LIBRARY - ORDER NOW!

SUPER SYSTEM *by Doyle Brunson.* This classic book is considered by the pros to be the best book ever written on poker! Jam-packed with advanced strategies, theories, tactics and money-making techniques, no serious poker player can afford to be without this hard-hitting information. Includes fifty pages of the most precise poker statistics ever published. Features chapters written by poker's biggest superstars, such as Dave Sklansky, Mike Caro, Chip Reese, Joey Hawthorne, Bobby Baldwin, and Doyle. Essential strategies, advanced play, and no-nonsense winning advice on making money at 7-card stud (razz, high-low split, cards speak, and declare), draw poker, lowball, and hold'em (limit and no-limit).This is a must-read for any serious poker player. 628 pages, $29.95.

SUPER SYSTEM 2 *by Doyle Brunson.* The most anticipated poker book ever, SS2 expands upon the original with more games and professional secrets from the best in the world. Superstar contributors include Daniel Negreanu, winner of multiple WSOP gold bracelets and 2004 Poker Player of the Year; Lyle Berman, 3-time WSOP gold bracelet winner, founder of the World Poker Tour, and super-high stakes cash player; Bobby Baldwin, 1978 World Champion; Johnny Chan, 2-time World Champion and 10-time WSOP bracelet winner; Mike Caro, poker's greatest researcher, theorist, and instructor; Jennifer Harman, the world's top female player and one of ten best overall; Todd Brunson, winner of more than 20 tournaments; and Crandell Addington, no-limit hold'em legend. 672 pgs, $34.95.

CARO'S GUIDE TO DOYLE BRUNSON'S SUPER SYSTEM *by Mike Caro.* Working with World Champion Doyle Brunson, the legendary Mike Caro has created a fresh look to the "Bible" of all poker books, adding new and personal insights that help you understand the original work. Caro breaks 36 concepts into either "Analysis, Commentary, Concept, Mission, Play-By-Play, Psychology, Statistics, Story, or Strategy. Lots of illustrations and winning concepts give even more value to this great work. 86 pages, 8 1/2 x 11, $19.95.

MY 50 MOST MEMORABLE HANDS *by Doyle Brunson.* Great players, legends, and poker's most momentous events march in and out of fifty years of unforgettable hands. Sit side-by-side with Doyle as he replays the excitement and life-changing moments of the most thrilling and crucial hands in the history of poker: from his early games as a rounder in the rough-and-tumble "Wild West" years—where a man was more likely to get shot as he was to get a straight flush—to the nail-biting excitement of his two world championship titles. Relive million dollar hands and the high stakes tension of sidestepping police, hijackers and murderers. A thrilling collection of stories and sage poker advice. 168 pages, $14.95.

THE POKER TOURNAMENT FORMULA *by Arnold Snyder.* Start making money now in fast no-limit hold'em tournaments with these radical and never-before-published concepts and secrets for beating tournaments. You'll learn why cards don't matter as much as the dynamics of a tournament—your position, the size of your chip stack, who your opponents are, and above all, the structure. Poker tournaments offer one of the richest opportunities to come along in decades. Every so often, a book comes along that changes the way players attack a game and provides them with a big advantage over opponents. Gambling legend Arnold Snyder has written such a book. 368 pages, $19.95.

POKER TOURNAMENT FORMULA 2: Advanced Strategies for Big Money Tournaments *by Arnold Snyder.* Probably the greatest tournament poker book ever written, and the most controversial in the last decade, Snyder's revolutionary work debunks commonly (and falsely) held beliefs. Snyder reveals the power of chip utility—the real secret behind winning tournaments—and covers utility ranks, tournament structures, small- and long-ball strategies, patience factors, the impact of structures, crushing the Harringbots and other player types, tournament phases, and much more. Includes big sections on Tools, Strategies, and Tournament Phases. A must buy! 496 pages, $24.95.

GREAT CARDOZA POKER BOOKS
ADD THESE TO YOUR LIBRARY - ORDER NOW!

CARO'S MOST PROFITABLE HOLD'EM ADVICE *by Mike Caro.* When Mike Caro writes a book on winning, all poker players take notice. And they should: The "Mad Genius of Poker" has influenced just about every professional player and world champion alive. You'll journey far beyond the traditional tactical tools offered in most poker books and for the first time, have access to the entire missing arsenal of strategies left out of everything you've ever seen or experienced. Caro's first major work in two decades is packed with hundreds of powerful ideas, concepts, and strategies, many of which will be new to you—they have never been made available to the general public. This book represents Caro's lifelong research into beating the game of hold em. 408 pages, $24.95

CARO'S BOOK OF POKER TELLS *by Mike Caro.* One of the ten greatest books written on poker, this must-have book should be in every player's library. If you're serious about winning, you'll realize that most of the profit comes from being able to read your opponents. Caro reveals the the secrets of interpreting *tells*—physical reactions that reveal information about a player's cards—such as shrugs, sighs, shaky hands, eye contact, and many more. Learn when opponents are bluffing, when they aren't and why—based solely on their mannerisms. Over 170 photos of players in action and play-by-play examples show the actual tells. These powerful ideas will give you the decisive edge. 320 pages, $24.95.

HOW TO BEAT SIT-AND-GO POKER TOURNAMENTS by Neil Timothy. There is a lot of dead money up for grabs in the lower limit sit-and-gos and Neil Timothy shows you how to go and get it. The author, a professional player, shows you how to reach the last six places of lower limit sit-and-go tournaments four out of five times and then how to get In the money 25-35 percent of the time using his powerful, proven strategies. This book can turn a losing sit-and-go player into a winner, and a winner into a bigger winner. Also effective for the early and middle stages of one-table satellites.176 pages, $14.95.

CHAMPIONSHIP NO-LIMIT & POT-LIMIT HOLD'EM *by T. J. Cloutier & Tom McEvoy.* The bible for winning pot-limit and no-limit hold'em tournaments gives you all the answers to your most important questions: How do you get inside your opponents' heads and learn how to beat them at their own game? How can you tell how much to bet, raise, and reraise in no-limit hold'em? When can you bluff? How do you set up your opponents in pot-limit hold'em so that you can win a monster pot? What are the best strategies for winning no-limit and pot-limit tournaments, satellites, and supersatellites? Inspired advice you can bank on from two of the most recognizable figures in poker. 304 pages, $29.95.

CHAMPIONSHIP HOLD'EM *by T. J. Cloutier & Tom McEvoy.* Hard-hitting hold'em the way it's played *today* in both limit cash games and tournaments. Get killer advice on how to win more money in rammin'-jammin' games, kill-pot, jackpot, shorthanded, and full table cash games. You'll learn the thinking process for preflop, flop, turn, and river play with specific suggestions for what to do when good or bad things happen. Includes play-by-play analyses, advice on how to maximize profits against rocks in tight games, weaklings in loose games, experts in solid games, plus tournament strategies for small buy-in, big buy-in, rebuy, add-on, satellite and major tournaments. Wow! 392 pages, $29.95.

CHAMPIONSHIP OMAHA (Omaha High-Low, Pot-limit Omaha, Limit High Omaha) *by Tom McEvoy & T.J. Cloutier.* Clearly-written strategies and powerful advice from Cloutier and McEvoy who have won four World Series of Poker Omaha titles. You'll learn how to beat low-limit and high-stakes games, play against loose and tight opponents, and the differing strategies for rebuy and freezeout tournaments. Learn the best starting hands, when slowplaying a big hand is dangerous, what danglers are (and why winners don't play them), why you sometimes fold the nuts on the flop and would be correct in doing so, and overall, how you can win a lot of money at Omaha! 296 pages, illustrations, $29.95.

POWERFUL WINNING POKER SIMULATIONS
A MUST FOR SERIOUS PLAYERS WITH A COMPUTER!
IBM compatible CD ROM Win 95, 98, 2000, NT, ME, XP

These incredible full color poker simulations are the best method to improve your game. Computer opponents play like real players. All games let you set the limits and rake and have fully programmable players, plus stat tracking, and Hand Analyzer for starting hands. MIke Caro, the world's foremost poker theoretician says, "Amazing... a steal for under $500... get it, it's great." Includes free phone support. "Smart Advisor" gives expert advice for every play!

1. TURBO TEXAS HOLD'EM FOR WINDOWS - $59.95. Choose which players, and how many (2-10) you want to play, create loose/tight games, and control check-raising, bluffing, position, sensitivity to pot odds, and more! Also, instant replay, pop-up odds, Professional Advisor keeps track of play statistics. Free bonus: Hold'em Hand Analyzer analyzes all 169 pocket hands in detail and their win rates under any conditions you set. Caro says this "hold'em software is the most powerful ever created." Great product!

2. TURBO SEVEN-CARD STUD FOR WINDOWS - $59.95. Create any conditions of play; choose number of players (2-8), bet amounts, fixed or spread limit, bring-in method, tight/loose conditions, position, reaction to board, number of dead cards, and stack deck to create special conditions. Features instant replay. Terrific stat reporting includes analysis of starting cards, 3-D bar charts, and graphs. Play interactively and run high speed simulation to test strategies. Hand Analyzer analyzes starting hands in detail. Wow!

3. TURBO OMAHA HIGH-LOW SPLIT FOR WINDOWS - $59.95. Specify any playing conditions; betting limits, number of raises, blind structures, button position, aggressiveness/passiveness of opponents, number of players (2-10), types of hands dealt, blinds, position, board reaction, and specify flop, turn, and river cards! Choose opponents and use provided point count or create your own. Statistical reporting, instant replay, pop-up odds high speed simulation to test strategies, amazing Hand Analyzer, and much more!

4. TURBO OMAHA HIGH FOR WINDOWS - $59.95. Same features as above, but tailored for Omaha High only. Caro says program is "an electrifying research tool...it can clearly be worth thousands of dollars to any serious player." A must for Omaha High players.

5. TURBO 7 STUD 8 OR BETTER - $59.95. Brand new with all the features you expect from the Wilson Turbo products: the latest artificial intelligence, instant advice and exact odds, play versus 2-7 opponents, enhanced data charts that can be exported or printed, the ability to fold out of turn and immediately go to the next hand, ability to peek at opponents hand, optional warning mode that warns you if a play disagrees with the advisor, and automatic mode that runs up to 50 tests unattended. Tough computer players vary their styles for a great game.

---

6. TOURNAMENT TEXAS HOLD'EM - $39.95
Set-up for tournament practice and play, this realistic simulation pits you against celebrity look-alikes. Tons of options let you control tournament size with 10 to 300 entrants, select limits, ante, rake, blind structures, freezeouts, number of rebuys and competition level of opponents. Pop-up status report shows how you're doing vs. the competition. Save tournaments in progress to play again later. Additional feature allows quick folds on finished hands.

Order now at 1-800-577-WINS or go online to: www.cardozabooks.com

303

FREE BOOK!
TAKE ADVANTAGE OF THIS OFFER NOW!

The book is **free**; the shipping is **free**. Truly, no obligation. Oops, we forgot. You also get a **free** catalog. **And a $10 off coupon!!** Mail in coupon below to get your free book or go to **www.cardozabooks.com** and click on the red OFFER button.

WHY ARE WE GIVING YOU THIS BOOK?
Why not? No, seriously, after more than 27 years as the world's foremost publisher of gaming books, we really appreciate your business. Take this **free** book as our thank you for being our customer; we're sure we'll see more of you!

THIS OFFER GETS EVEN BETTER & BETTER!
You'll get a **FREE** catalog of all our products—over 200 to choose from—and get this: you'll also get a **$10 FREE** coupon good for purchase of <u>any</u> product in our catalog! Our offer is pretty simple. Let me sum it up for you:
1. Order your **FREE** book
2. Shipping of your book is **FREE!***
3. Get a **FREE** catalog (over 200 items—and more on the web)
4. You <u>also</u> get a **$10 OFF** coupon good for anything we sell
5. Enjoy your free book and **WIN**!

CHOOSE YOUR FREE BOOK
Choose one book from any in the Basics of Winning Series (15 choices): Baccarat, Bingo, Blackjack, Bridge, Caribbean Stud Poker and Let it Ride, Chess, Craps, Hold'em, Horseracing, Keno, Lotto/Lottery, Poker, Roulette, Slots, Sports Betting, Video Poker.

Or choose one book from here: Internet Hold'em Poker, Crash Course in Beating Texas Hold'em, Poker Talk, Poker Tournament Tips from the Pros, or any other title listed.

When you order your free book by Internet, enter the coupon code **KWTHE2**.

HURRY! GET YOUR FREE BOOK NOW!
USE THIS COUPON OR GO TO OUR WEBSITE!
YES! Send me my **FREE** book! I understand there is no obligation! Send coupon to:Cardoza Publishing, P.O. Box 98115, Las Vegas, NV 89193. <u>No</u> phone calls please.

Free book by website: www.cardozabooks.com (click on red OFFER button)

*Shipping is FREE to U.S. (Sorry, due to very high ship costs, we cannot offer this outside the U.S. However, we still have good news for foreign customers: Spend $25 or more with us and we'll include that free book for you anyway!)

WRITE IN FREE BOOK HERE _____

Name _____

Address_____

City _____ State _____ Zip _____

Email Address* _____ Coupon Code: <u>KWTHE2</u>

*Get our FREE newsletter and special offers when you provide your email. Your information is <u>protected</u> by our privacy guarantee: We've been in business 27 years and do NOT and never have sold customer info. One coupon per address or per person only. Offer subject to cancellation at any time.